—Holly Smith's—
M£☺NEY
SAVING
BO✂K

Holly Smith's

MONEY SAVING BOOK

Simple saving hacks for a happy life

EBURY
PRESS

To my social media community and bargain-hunting Facebook members, without you this book wouldn't be possible.

About the author

Holly Smith is a mum-of-three, a trusted bargain hunter and money-saving social media influencer. She's the founder of the Extreme Couponing and Bargains UK Facebook page and group which have a combined following of 2.5 million. She lives in Great Yarmouth with her husband, Callum, and their three young children.

Holly can be found on YouTube, TikTok and Instagram, helping as many people as possible to save money.

YouTube www.youtube.com/hollyvlogsofficial
Instagram/Twitter @HollyVlogs
TikTok @hollyvlogsofficial

CONTENTS

How I got into money saving (and how you can do it too)

✋ *Hi, I'm Holly. You might know me from my YouTube channel Holly Vlogs, TikTok or my Facebook group, Extreme Couponing and Bargains UK. Even if you haven't come across me on social media, there's one important thing that you need to know. I love a good bargain and money saving is my passion. I especially love helping other people to save money.*

• •

Money saving has always been my escape, especially during hard times. As a child, I got bullied at school. I was the 'weird one', the loner who sat on her own in the corner. I didn't know how to play with other children or join in and I felt different to everyone else.

My escape was going grocery shopping with my mum to our local Safeway supermarket. Handheld scanners had just come in and I was fascinated seeing all of the packets and tins get scanned and their prices pop up. My parents were extremely frugal and were always trying to save money, so I used to memorise the prices and help Mum to find the cheapest products.

As I got older, the bullying got worse. I was an easy target and it was mental and physical. By the time I was fourteen, it got too much. I didn't want to go to school any more so I was homeschooled. I was so scared of seeing the bullies that I didn't leave my house for a whole year.

Over time, I tried to build up my confidence and one day my friends persuaded me to go with them to use the Internet at the local library. All my nightmares came true when I saw one of the school bullies. She walked over and punched me in the mouth. The force was so severe, every bone in my upper jaw was broken and the only thing that kept my teeth in place was my metal brace.

The incident destroyed any confidence that I had left, and I was too scared to leave the house again. To pass the time, I got obsessed with a website called Swapitshop — it was a bit like eBay for kids. You would list your product and another member would buy it for points. You collected points and bought things you wanted. I was good at it and I went into charity shops and bought stuff at a bargain price that I knew I could sell for more online.

At seventeen, I rebelled! I ran away from home with a boy who was four years older than me. We had no money and lived in a caravan. We sold second-hand goods and DVDs at car boot sales to try to make enough to pay our rent. Each week it was a struggle to be able to afford to feed ourselves, and every penny counted. Everything I'd learnt from shopping with my mum as a kid, I put into practice and I shopped around to find the best bargains.

I still didn't know what I wanted to do with my life. I'd started so many college courses including performing arts, beauty therapy and hairdressing but I had to give them all up because I couldn't interact with people.

After seven years, I realised I wasn't happy in the relationship, so I left. After another failed relationship, I met Callum at a martial arts school. I thought he was way out of my league, and I was too scared to ask him out, so my friend arranged a double date with his mate. The date was terrible — my friend got really drunk and was sick in the pub — but Callum and I started seeing each other.

My health had never been good. I'd started getting crippling pains in my leg and one day I collapsed. It turned out I had a tumour in the bone. Thankfully it wasn't cancerous, and I had surgery to remove it.

Throughout my teens I'd also been rushed to hospital several times with agonising stomach pains and they'd got worse. To distract myself from the pain, I started entering competitions. I entered 300 every week and I won £10,000 in prizes in a year including £3,500 in cash. I'd started an apprenticeship in animal care, so this was my income and I sold some of the prizes I'd won on eBay. Money was still tight, and I'd also got into couponing. I have a photographic memory so when I did a food shop, the price of every item was in my head and I instinctively knew a good bargain when I saw one.

Finally, I was diagnosed with endometriosis and had three operations, but I was devastated to be told that I might struggle to have kids. The one thing I wanted to be in life was a mum, so Callum and I started trying for a baby. I was distraught when the months went by and it didn't happen, even with the help of fertility drugs. I was put on the waiting list for IVF and then a few weeks later I found out I was pregnant. I was twenty-five when I had Mollie and six months later Callum and I got married.

My life was going well but personally I was really struggling. Callum had lots of friends, but I found it difficult to socialise, so I would never go out with them. I struggled with meeting new people and they'd think I was rude because I couldn't do small talk. I went to see the doctor and was eventually referred to an autism specialist. The day I got the official diagnosis was the best day ever. It gave me more confidence because I could explain to someone why I struggled when I was in a social situation. Mostly I felt relief that it wasn't my fault that I'd been bullied and attacked. It wasn't because I was a weirdo or a horrible person, I was autistic.

Eighteen months later, I had my second daughter, Bella. Now I had my own family to feed, I saved money where I could. If I could save one or two pounds or get something for free or cheap with a coupon then I would. I'd put the money that I'd saved aside so that one day we could go on a family holiday.

I was still entering competitions and I'd joined a local competition club. Eight of us would meet up for a cup of tea and a biscuit and talk about the prizes we'd won. I was particularly close to a lady in her fifties called Sue whose family had nicknamed her, Voucher Vera. She called me the Coupon Queen because of all the money I had saved, and she was always really encouraging.

I was devastated when Sue was diagnosed with terminal cancer. The last time I saw her, she made me promise that I would start a money-saving business. 'You're a natural, you need your own blog,' she told me. But I didn't have a clue where to start.

The night after Sue's funeral, I went home to find an email telling me I'd won a competition. The prize was for a web designer to make me my own blog and website. I couldn't help but think it was meant to be and that was where my first blog UK Couponing started. I went on to set up a Facebook page too. I'd look after the girls during the day and at night

I'd scour the Internet for good deals, offers and coupons that I could share, and I'd track prices online. After six months I had 20,000 followers. All my family and friends came to me if they wanted to book a holiday or go out for a meal because they knew I'd always find ways to save them money.

There was an American TV show called *Extreme Couponing* where people competed to get the most shopping for free using money-saving coupons. People said it couldn't be done in the UK, but I was determined to prove them wrong. In December 2015, I did a record-breaking supermarket shop where I got £1,200 worth of shopping for free using coupons, which I then donated to charity.

Through all of this I was still getting agonising stomach pains. The doctors thought it was my gall bladder, so I had that removed, then I developed a rare condition and had to have more surgery. However, I got pancreatitis and spent six weeks fighting for my life in hospital. The one thing that kept me going was saving money! I got Callum to bring my laptop into the hospital and I kept myself distracted by finding bargains for people online.

I was still determined to find out what was wrong with me and I went to see so many doctors and specialists. I found one who thought my constant pain was connected to acid reflux and suggested surgery to help but during the operation my liver was damaged. Over the next few days I got more and more ill until I fell unconscious and had to have emergency surgery to save my life. I spent another six weeks in Intensive Care.

Even when I'd recovered, the pain hadn't gone away, and at times it left me screaming in agony. I found a specialist in London who agreed to see me and finally I was diagnosed with a rare autoimmune condition called Mast Cell

Activation Disorder. It was such a relief to finally have an answer and I was put on a trial drug. It had always been my big dream to take the girls to Disney World. I'd been saving up for years, but I'd never been well enough to go. Over the next nine months we went twice, and I had the best holidays of my life. I also hit a million followers on my Facebook page.

Unfortunately, in 2019 I got a third bone tumour in my leg. The doctor didn't know why they kept coming back, but he removed it and filled up the bone with concrete. It means I walk with a limp now and sometimes, if I'm on my feet all day, I have to use a crutch.

A month after the surgery I was shocked to find out I was pregnant. I was told I wouldn't be able to have any more children but the trial drug I'd been put on had been found to boost fertility! Our gorgeous son, Cloud, was born in November 2019.

Throughout all the ups and downs, money saving has been my saviour. Thinking about the savings I could share to help other people really kept me going and occupied my mind during tough and painful times.

After a while, I was asked to speak at events and businesses wanted to advertise on my website. Now I get to do what I love and make an income from it. Autism is my superpower. When I see a price, it stays in my head and I'm constantly researching how to find the best bargains.

My message to you is if I can do it, anybody can. I was told by doctors to go home and live on benefits for the rest of my life because there was nothing else I could do. But there is always hope. Now more than ever, I know money is a constant struggle for some people and I've been there myself. But things will always get better.

What's in this book?

I wanted to share my story of how I've saved my family thousands of pounds in the hope that you can do it too along with some of the best ideas from the money-saving community. So as well my hacks, this book features over 100 brilliant hacks and tips from the members of the Extreme Couponing and Bargains UK Facebook group. With a community of over 1.4 million people, when it comes to saving money, my members really know their stuff. I've included the hacks that have gone viral and have had millions of comments and 'likes' on the group. They are all simple, useful, life-changing tips and tricks that really will help. The ingenious things my members come up with never cease to amaze me. Thank you to every member. You all help to create such a brilliant, supportive online community.

This book also features over fifty expert hacks from some of the UK's top social media influencers who I'm lucky enough to also call my friends. Each of them are experts in their own field, so whether it's saving money at Christmas, on your food shop or a holiday or how to make money as a YouTuber or TikTok star, these guys have the answers for you.

People have asked me for this book for a long time. It's all of my best advice in one handy place and I hope it not only gives you the tools to save yourself some money, but that it even helps you make some extra cash along the way too. So have a read and let me know how much you've managed to save.

Love

Holly x

SAVING MONEY

➜ From slashing the price of your food shop and your monthly bills to being able to enjoy a day out, a holiday and even Christmas without breaking the bank, this section is where I share all my best money-saving hints, tips and tricks. I'll show you how I do it and I can guarantee that you will soon notice the difference.

How to slash your supermarket spend

After paying your mortgage or rent, most people's biggest monthly expense is their food bill, so if you can save on that, it makes a real difference. I absolutely love shopping for groceries. I still remember going to the supermarket with my mum as a kid and helping her find the cheapest items. I do my research, go to lots of different shops and hunt out the best bargains. But I know not everyone has the time and some people want the convenience of going to one store for their weekly shop. Even if you do just go to one place, there are still ways that you can save yourself money. Whichever supermarket you shop in, follow my simple money-saving tips and eventually they'll become habits. You'll soon notice the difference when you get to the checkout.

• •

 BEFORE YOU GO SHOPPING

There are a few simple things you can do before you go to the supermarket:

Make a shopping list based around meals

Plan your meals for the week and put all the ingredients you need on your shopping list. I know if I don't have a list, I end up buying random stuff and then struggle to know what to cook. If you can, double up on ingredients for recipes and batch cook some extra portions to put in your freezer. Food that's in season tends to be a lot cheaper than food that isn't. Use Google to find out what food is in season and then search for recipes and meal plan around those.

Check the prices online

Before you go shopping, check online to see what offers and deals are on in the supermarket that you're going to. You might have beef mince on your list because you want to make a Bolognese sauce but then you might look online and see there's an offer on lamb mince so change your meal to a moussaka. Adapt your meal plan and list depending on the promotions at the supermarket. Doing a little bit of prep before you go will save you money in the long run.

Take cash

If you're an impulse buyer, then my number one tip is to take cash and not cards. At the time of writing, some stores were not accepting cash because of the Covid pandemic. But if you can pay with cash, I think it is one of the easiest ways to limit your spending to your budget. It's all about training yourself to shop differently. If you have £100 cash to spend on groceries, then you're not going to pick up impulse buys because you don't want to be embarrassed at the checkout if you haven't got enough money on you. Shopping with cash makes you more mindful and less likely to pick up things you don't need.

AT THE SUPERMARKET

As soon as you step into a supermarket and start walking down the aisles, all those good intentions (and your budget!)

are often easily forgotten. So, here are some quick, easy things that you can do when you go food shopping that I guarantee will save you cash.

Don't buy pre-prepared

Don't buy bags or cartons of already chopped fruit and veg — you're paying for convenience. For example, in most supermarkets you'll get a whole iceberg lettuce for around 50p but a bag of sliced iceberg lettuce, that's half the amount, usually costs double. Chop them up yourself at home — it takes minutes — or buy a food processor which will pay for itself several times over with the money that you'll save by chopping your own food.

Buy loose

Buy fruit and veg loose and not pre-packed. A pre-packed bag of bananas will cost around £1 but if you buy them loose it usually works out at half the price. Most supermarkets have digital weighing scales so you can check the cost of loose fruit and veg. I also find that buying cheese from the deli counter can be cheaper than buying it from the cheese aisle. The only exception to this rule is potatoes which tend to work out cheaper if you buy them bagged.

Buy wonky

To prevent waste, some of the leading supermarkets like Asda, Morrisons and Tesco now sell boxes of imperfect or 'wonky' fruit and veg for a fraction of the cost. They're brilliant value — you normally pay between £1 and £3 for a good-sized box of misshapen items that in the past would have been thrown away. You'll find them in the fruit and veg aisles, but they tend to sell out very quickly.

Big isn't always best

Buying the bigger pack isn't always the best value for money. Always look at the price labels in supermarkets which tell you how much you're paying according to weight. My husband Callum loves doing this when we go shopping. Something might be in a bigger package or carton but when you look at the actual weight inside, it's half full! Sometimes it works out cheaper to buy two smaller packs instead of one larger size. It's worth spending a little extra time looking at labels as it really will pay off.

Opt for own brands

So many people snub supermarket own-brand products, but I think they're a no-brainer, especially when it comes to basics like pasta and rice, tinned fruit and items you're going to use frequently as ingredients in sauces, soups and stews like tinned tomatoes. In fact, a lot of own-brand products are made in the same factory as brand names, you're just paying more for the packaging and marketing. It's worth giving them a try and working out what you do or don't like. I used to buy Heinz ketchup but one day I picked up Asda's own brand for 30p and my kids love it. I know some people might be embarrassed to have own-brand ketchup bottles when guests come round but you can always be cheeky and pour the cheap stuff into a brand-name bottle or a clear glass jar or bottle that you've got lying around at home.

Ignore pink packaging

Don't be fooled by toiletries marketed specifically for women. Often you're paying way over the odds for the same product just because it's in pretty pink packaging. If you need a razor or shaving foam, then look in the men's section as you'll usually find the same products much cheaper. In one of my most popular TikTok videos I show a five pack of pink razors from a well-known brand which cost £1.30. But in the men's aisle a ten pack of the <u>exact same razors</u> (made in the same factory) was £1.

Beware of BOGOF

To increase sales, supermarkets always have lots of offers on, such as BOGOF (buy one, get one free) and three for two. But always check that you're getting a good deal by checking the usual price online. I often find that supermarkets increase the price of products before putting them on promotion. If a BOGOF is a genuine saving, then it's a good time to stock up on items that you use regularly.

Use the barcode scanners

Most of the leading supermarkets have barcode scanners in their larger stores and as well as saving time at the checkout, they're a great way to keep track of what you're buying. If you have a barcode scanner, you're more conscious of what you're putting in your trolley and you can keep an eye on your running total. Too many people get to the checkout and are shocked at how much they've spent, but then it's too late. If they don't have scanners in the store that you're shopping in, some supermarkets like Tesco and Asda have an app that enables you to scan things and keep track of your running total although you can't use them to pay at the tills. Or you can use a calculator on your phone to keep track of what you're spending.

Buy frozen

You don't always have to buy fresh. Frozen fruit and veg is a lot cheaper and is just as nutritious.

Check the specialist food aisles

If you need plain rice, lentils or spices then look in the specialist food aisles as you'll often find it cheaper there. Most leading supermarkets will have sections devoted to certain cuisines like Indian, Polish, Chinese and Thai. You'll often find the food in these sections comes in bigger bags and is better value for money than the same items in other aisles.

Get a meal deal

Look for in-store meal deals. All of the leading supermarkets do them and they vary in price — you can pick up a frozen food meal deal at the Co-op for £5. My favourite is M&S as they have a good range of gluten-free options, you get a main course, side, dessert and a bottle of wine for £10 and the wine alone is normally £10. I save the wine for Christmas presents!

Bring your own bags

Don't forget to bring your own carrier bags when you go shopping. Even though they're only around 10p, this adds up over time and you end up with an endless supply of bags in your house. I use a Sass & Belle reusable bag, which folds up into a keyring, so it means I always have a bag to hand.

THE SALES 'TRICKS'

Go higher or lower

Supermarkets put the most expensive products at eye level. You tend to find all the pricey branded items in the middle of the shelves in the hope that you'll see them first and put them in your trolley. So always look higher up on the shelf and lower down because you'll find the cheaper products there.

Leave the kids at home

I know it's not always possible but, if you can, don't shop with your kids as supermarkets know how to target them. For example, sweets at the checkout are placed at a lower level so children will see them and they're often the most expensive ones. A single KitKat at the tills might be 70p but you'll find a pack of four in the aisles for £1. There's also special limited-edition packaging that appeals to kids — like unicorns and dinosaurs —and costs more even though it's the same product inside. Not to mention the rides at the end of the checkouts that your kids will beg you for a go on!

Don't go shopping hungry

It's an obvious one but we all still fall into it. Supermarkets want to tempt you, so they'll put fresh bakery items like donuts right by the entrance and suddenly you'll think 'Hmm, I fancy one of them' and chuck them in your trolley. Some supermarkets even pump in smells like freshly baked bread and cakes to try to entice you to buy them.

Stick to what you've come for

When I was a kid I went to the supermarket with my mum and all you could buy was food. Now you go to the supermarket and you can buy so many other things — toys, homeware, clothes . . . When you step foot in a store it's like an obstacle course as there are so many things laid in your path to tempt you. If you're trying to save money, then focus on what you came to buy. Supermarket store planners know you're a captive market so they'll do everything they can to keep you in the store for longer in the hope that you'll spend more. They'll even move sections to different places in the store so you'll have to walk up and down the aisles to find them and be more tempted to buy things that you don't need.

Supermarket hacks

If you're at the supermarket and you **need a trolley,** but you don't have a trolley token, or a pound, just use two 20ps stacked on top of each other. It works just the same for most trolleys.

Some supermarkets have **student shopping cards**. They come as a pack of two — one for the student and one for parents — which you pick up free in store. Parents can load up their card with money which will then automatically go onto the student's card so they can use it for their weekly groceries. It's great for parents as, unlike giving cash to students, they have the reassurance that the money on the card can only be spent in the supermarket they choose.

Bake a cake for less than £1. Buy a packet of supermarket own brand cake mix and add either a value tin of sliced peaches or pineapple to the mix to get a nice fruity cake.

When you're **buying medication,** such as cold and flu remedies, check out the product licence (PL) number on the packaging. Products that have the same PL number have exactly the same ingredients and are made in the same factory, but you'll pay much more for branded products. So always go for own brand when it comes to buying medication.

Fill up your freezer because it's cheaper to run than one that's half empty. A half-empty freezer uses more energy to cool items down and tends to burn out quicker because it's doing more work. So, bulk-buying food to freeze and batch cooking are good options for keeping your freezer topped up. If you're worried about a power cut, then most home insurance policies cover frozen food up to the value of £100.

If you drink wine, it's worth joining **wine clubs,** such as Naked Wines and Laithwaite's, as you can get some really good savings when you buy in bulk.

EXPERT HACKS!

Kelly, who blogs at **reducedgrub.com,** wanted to share this gem:

Never go shopping when you've just been paid. It's too tempting to put so many extras into your trolley.

AMAZING MEMBERS' HACKS

'Eat vegetarian meals for two days a week. This has saved me over £300 this year alone. Meat's expensive compared to meals which you can substitute with vegetables and lentils.'

'Freeze all your leftovers no matter how small. They make a great base for another meal.'

'If you have an iPhone, use the reminders app to make a list for food shopping. Share it with your partner and you can both edit and add to it.'

'Write a meal plan for the week, check your cupboards to see what you might need to buy then do an online shop. I just almost halved my bill by doing that, from £100 to £57.'

'I'm constantly throwing away cling film as it gets too sticky and I can't unroll it properly. Then someone told me to keep it in the fridge. It stops it sticking together when you're trying to use it.'

'Grow your own herbs at home, such as mint and basil. This saves me a lot of money as I just cut off the leaves I want when I need to use them in a recipe.'

'Save waste and don't store potatoes near onions or they will spoil quicker.'

My food-shopping secrets 🐷

When it comes to buying groceries, I always shop around. If you do all of your shopping at one supermarket, you're paying for the convenience of having everything in one place. To really save money, you need to shop around and here's how to do it.

• •

Buy brands from bargain stores

I buy all of my tins, packets and jars in discount shops like Home Bargains and B&M. They sell lots of branded products much cheaper than the supermarkets and this is where I stock up on all of mine and my kids' favourite brands like Baxters soups, Dolmio pasta sauce and Heinz beans. I absolutely LOVE Uncle Ben's curry sauce and, at the time of writing this, it's £2.50 in Tesco but in Home Bargains it's £1 for exactly the same product.

The reasons bargain stores are cheaper than the supermarkets . . .
- Products could be coming up to (or even be past) their best before date.
- The packaging contains an old promotion or a competition that has expired.
- It's a seasonal item. For example, Cadbury Creme Eggs aren't sold in supermarkets after Easter, but discount

stores buy the excess stock from supermarkets to resell at a low price.

☺ The products are made especially for discount retailers. For example, you can buy a six-pack of Walkers Crisps in supermarkets for £2 but you can buy a five-pack of Walkers Crisps in bargain stores for £1.

Some of the larger branches of these discount stores also have a fresh food section where you can buy fruit, veg and meat a lot cheaper than in the supermarkets. One of my regular purchases is 500g of lean beef mince which is currently £2.49 at my local Home Bargains but I'd pay £4 for the same product if I bought it from a leading supermarket.

Best-before bargains

People often get confused by 'use by' and 'best before' dates. All fresh foods, such as meat and dairy products, have a use-by date and it's illegal for retailers to sell food past that date. But food labelled 'best before' can be eaten AFTER its best before date and there are specialist online retailers who sell this food for a fraction of the cost. Even items like toilet rolls, toiletries and alcohol have a best before date. Some of the most well-known websites include:
approvedfood.co.uk
clearancexl.co.uk
cutpricebarrys.co.uk

Buying food past or coming up to its best before date can save you a fortune and I use these websites to stock up on items like crisps for my girls' packed lunches and things that we use regularly, such as cooking sauces. Some people might turn their noses up at this, but Callum and I have ordered from many of these retailers and, I have to say, we've found that anything that's within six months after its best before date has tasted fine. Even after six months, things like crisps taste a bit different but they're still perfectly edible! You can pick up some great bargains – I've bought bottles of Heinz and Hellmann's sauces for just a penny each and ten packets of KP crisps for £1.

A lot of people buy food past its best before date, pay full price for it and don't even realise. I once found a packet of Hobnobs in a leading supermarket that were over a year old!

Buy in bulk

If you can afford to buy in bulk from a wholesaler like Costco or Makro it can save you a heck of a lot of money. If you can't afford to buy in bulk on your own or you haven't got the room at home to store it, then split your shopping with friends and family. To shop at Costco, you need to be a member and buy an annual subscription which varies from £15 for online shopping only to £74 for an individual executive subscription. Check the website to see if you meet the list of membership criteria.

I go to Makro wholesale cash and carry. To be able to shop there you need to be a company or self-employed (and be able to prove it) to get a Makro trade card membership. Check the website for details and to see if you qualify.

Some of the frozen food stores such as Farmfoods also do good bulk-buy offers on non-frozen items. I recently picked up 24 cans of Pepsi Max from Iceland Food Warehouse for £5.99 that I shared with my dad.

Go to the budget supermarkets

You can generally make much bigger savings by shopping in budget supermarkets like Aldi and Lidl rather than in the leading supermarkets. You can still get some brand names and they also do their own dupes of brands that are often very similar. But one word of warning — beware of the middle aisle! I made a meme once about going into Aldi for groceries and coming out with a two-man tent — it went viral because it's true! Stuff might be cheap but that doesn't mean that you need it. My dad once went into Lidl for some shopping and came out with a set of power tools even though he already had two of them at home. He didn't need it, but he bought it because it was only £20 and they're normally around £60. We've all fallen for it but you're not going to save money if you get waylaid by the middle of Lidl or the special buys in Aldi.

Look for the yellow stickers

Every day, supermarkets reduce fresh food coming up to its use-by date and put a yellow sticker on it. Each store is different, but they'll generally start doing the first reductions around 5pm which are normally 20%. If the products haven't sold a couple of hours later, they'll take 50% off. Once it gets to 9pm, you can sometimes get up to 90% off. All supermarkets are different, so the next time you're in your local store ask a member of staff when they start reducing fresh food and where they tend to put it. Yellow-sticker items are great to buy and put in your freezer (remember you can freeze bread, milk and cheese as well as meat and fish), but please be respectful to the supermarket staff. So many times, I've seen shoppers snatch reduced things out of their hands or grab them off of a moving trolley.

Try a food waste app

These apps, which originated in America, are such a great idea and are becoming more popular in the UK. The Too Good to Go app lets you buy unsold food from cafes, bakeries and restaurants at massively reduced prices that otherwise would be thrown away at the end of the day. You can get some amazing deals, especially if you live in a city where there are a lot of eateries. You can get everything from cakes and sandwiches to kebabs and whole restaurant meals. My best bargain was getting a box of donuts for 10p. After signing up, you use an interactive map to select what you want, pay via the app and then you collect your meal within a certain time frame. You have to be quick as things tend to go very quickly and there's a certain element of chance about what you'll get as it depends on what's surplus that day. Members on my Facebook groups have picked up some incredible bargains including large boxes of fruit and veg from Morrisons, huge trays of sushi from YO! Sushi and mixed bags of pastries from Greggs and Caffè Nero all for around £3.

Olio is another food waste app where individuals can give away free food that they're not going to use. It can be stuff that they've bought, grown or even cooked. It also tends to go extremely quickly, so you need to check the app regularly.

Sign up to a meal subscription box

Meal subscription boxes like Hello Fresh, Gousto and Mindful Chef are worth a try but only if you can get them on offer. They take the hassle out of meal planning and they come with everything that you need so there's no waste. We tend to get one every couple of weeks. You normally get 50% off your first month so I take advantage of that offer and then I cancel it when it runs out and switch to another company. After a couple of weeks, they'll send you a new offer to try to entice you back. So, I take advantage of that multiple times, cancel it again and then leave and go back to another company. They work out a lot more affordable if you can always buy them on offer. You can sometimes refer friends for discounts too. I once referred ten friends to Gousto and got free food boxes for a month.

Save cash on gluten-free and vegan products

I'm gluten-free and I'm always outraged at how the prices of the 'free from' items are hiked up. So instead of shopping in the expensive gluten-free aisles, I use apps such as Gluten Free Scanner, Food Scanner and GF Plate to scan items in the regular aisles to see what's gluten-free. You'd be surprised at how many products you find and you're not paying over the odds for them.

There are also apps like Vegan Scanner that tell you which food is vegan but might not be marketed specifically as such. Did you know for example that beef and tomato Pot Noodles are actually vegan?! If you can't substitute an item in the gluten-free aisle (such as bread), then sign-up to gluten-free clubs which are run by GF brands as they regularly send out freebies and promotions.

Food-shop hacks

If you shop regularly in B&M, **it's worth downloading the B&M app** on to your smartphone as it has a barcode scanner function. Everything that's out of range and they need to get rid of tends to be heavily reduced (sometimes as low as 10p). The staff might not have had a chance to update the price labels yet, but your app will tell you the discounted price. I've picked up so many bargains this way including board games and great toys for 10p. Sometimes if I'm in B&M and I've got

Holly's **HACKS**

a bit of time on my hands, I'll scan a few items just to see if there are any bargains to be had. You'll be surprised at what you might find.

If you've recently been diagnosed as **gluten free**, register for a free taster box at www.glutafin.co.uk which includes GF recipes and free samples of GF food.

Save the recipe cards from your meal subscription boxes so you can make the meals again, using your own ingredients.

AMAZING MEMBERS' HACKS

'Buy meat in bulk online. I ordered a Muscle Food hamper and it saved me loads. It works out good value and is delivered directly to your door.'

'Write "use-by" dates on your calendar so you know what food has got to be used by when.'

How to be a savvy shopper online and offline

Whether you're shopping online, like many of us now do, or in store there are lots of apps, tips and tricks that you can use to save you money. Here are some of my favourites.

• •

Use cashback websites

When you're buying something online, use cashback websites, such as TopCashback and Quidco, where you earn commission on your online purchases. You log on to the site and search the retailer where you want to shop. You then go on to their website and that link will keep track of what you buy, and you'll earn a percentage back. It only takes a few clicks and when you reach £20 you can either cash out with a gift voucher or the money can be paid into your bank account. I use these sites every time I shop online as it's an easy way to make money.

Buy or sell unwanted gift cards

You can get some great discounts by buying unwanted gift cards on websites, such as cardyard.co.uk. If you know that you're going to buy something from a particular retailer then it's well worth it particularly if it's a voucher that's nearing its expiry date. For example, my girls love Build-a-Bear so I could pick up a £100 gift card on there for just £70. You know they're all legit because the company checks each card is loaded and they verify it before they go on sale as well as stating the expiry date. You can also sell gift cards that you're not going to use. You send the gift card to the company, then they check the balance on it and keep a small percentage of the fee when it's sold.

THE QUICKEST WAYS TO FIND THE BEST PRICE FOR AN ONLINE ITEM

- ☺ Use price comparison websites, such as pricespy.co.uk, kelkoo.co.uk, pricerunner.com and idealo.co.uk to check the best price before you buy so you don't have to search through every retailer's website manually.
- ☺ Type the barcode of the item you want to buy into Google to compare the prices at different retailers. Or type in the model number and it will bring them up in Google shopping. Always check the delivery price too as that can bump up the cost.

Get a head start on the sales

Be alerted to when your favourite retailers are having a sale by signing up to websites, such as lovesales.com. You create a watch list and they let you know when a sale is starting.

Sign up for newsletters

Some brands send discounts codes to new customers when you sign up for their newsletters. You'll also be notified of sales and promotions and possibly be sent discount codes for your birthday.

Price promise

Some retailers like John Lewis have a price policy that means if you see the same product being sold by another high-street competitor for a lower price, they'll refund you the difference. It has to be within twenty-eight days of you buying the item from them.

Check if there's a discount code

Before you buy something from a retailer, do a quick search on Google to see if there's a discount code available. A much easier and quicker way though is to download a Google Chrome plugin such as Honey or Pouch. When you're on a website and go to check out, they'll go through every single discount code that could possibly work for that retailer and automatically apply the code(s) to your basket within seconds. Sometimes it's even possible to use multiple discount codes on one purchase. They're brilliant as they do all the hard work for you, so you don't have to manually search for codes.

Join money-saving Facebook groups

Join Facebook groups like mine (Extreme Couponing and Bargains UK) where people share the bargains that they've found both online and in stores.

Refer your friends

Some websites will give you money off when you refer your friends and they make a purchase. It's normally something like '£5 off your next order' but some high-end websites, such as Charlotte Tilbury will give you up to £20 off your next purchase (sometimes a minimum spend applies). Refer your friends around peak times, such as Christmas when they're more likely to buy something.

BUYING HIGH-VALUE ELECTRICAL ITEMS

☺ Always check the guarantee as some companies offer longer ones than others. John Lewis and Richer Sounds are particularly good.

☺ If you're buying a big item in-store then don't be afraid to haggle. There's often wiggle room, so it's worth asking nicely if there's any discount on offer if you were to buy the item today. Even if they can't give you money off, they might chuck something else in like free software with a computer or another remote control for a TV. Put your embarrassment to one side and have a cheeky ask. It's worth a try and I've never been turned down.

☺ It's also worth asking if there's a display model of the item that you want to buy, as often they'll give it to you at a cheaper price if it's due to come off display.

How to get a genuine bargain on Black Friday

Black Friday comes from America. It's the Friday after Thanksgiving in late November when the retailers traditionally have their sales. For some reason, about five years ago someone decided to bring this to the UK and there were a lot of staged PR events by the stores where actors pretended to crush each other in a rush to get bargains. Black Friday now seems to run across a whole week in the UK and you can get some amazing bargains. But you can also get a load of rubbish that you don't need.

My best advice is, think before you buy. Would you have bought this item in the first place? Don't buy something just because it's 70% off or it's cheap. I've seen so many unwanted foot spas at car boot sales over the years!

If there are some high-end brands that you love, then Black Friday can be a good time to take advantage of some great promotions. I love Charlotte Tilbury make-up and on previous Black Fridays the website has sold mystery boxes that contain £350 worth of products for £80. There are only a limited amount available, so I make sure I'm signed up to all the notifications for when they go on sale. I focus on limited edition offers and the more exclusive brands that don't normally go on sale at any other time of the year.

If you want to buy something in particular like a TV, do your research beforehand. Find a few models that you want and check their prices before Black Friday, then you can see if you're getting a genuine bargain.

Some retailers use Black Friday to offer good discount codes across the whole store which is always worth taking advantage of. For example, The Entertainer toy store normally does a 20% off code so it's a good time to get newer toys that don't normally go on offer for Christmas presents.

LOYALTY CARDS AND SCHEMES

They're always worth signing up to, even if you don't shop at that particular store a lot, and many of them have an accompanying app. Set up a dedicated email address especially for cards and schemes. That way you're not bombarded with newsletters, but you can check it every now and again to see if there's an offer on at the retailer that you want to visit.

I used to hate rummaging around in my purse at the till trying to find my loyalty cards. Now you don't have to as there are apps like Stocard that store all your cards for you virtually. When you get to the till, you search the app for the card that you want, and the cashier scans the barcode from your smartphone.

But remember loyalty doesn't always pay. If you have a Tesco Clubcard and you go there every single week they know you're loyal so they're unlikely to send you many promotions. But if I stop shopping at my local Tesco for a few weeks then suddenly I'll get six weeks of coupons through my door trying to entice me back. So, I go back for a few weeks and once I've used the coupons up, then I go and shop somewhere else.

Loyalty cards can track when you've stopped shopping and they want you back. If you have one, it's worth trying to shop somewhere other than your usual supermarket for a while and see what happens.

COUPONING

Couponing and discount vouchers were one of the reasons I got into money saving. Seven years ago, I watched a US TV show called *Extreme Couponing* and I thought 'why am I not doing that?' I realised just how much you could save on your shop with coupons and I made it my mission to find as many coupons as I could. I still hold the record for the UK's biggest supermarket shop using coupons!

Couponing is still around although it's mainly virtual now because people were taking advantage by photocopying coupons and using them multiple times. The supermarkets were losing thousands of pounds a week because they weren't able to recoup their money from the brands. Once you redeem a digital coupon, you can't reuse it. Also, there are not as many coupons around today but if you can get your hands on them, they're still a great way to save cash.

Where to find coupons

⊚ Download a digital coupon app, such as Shopmium, ClickSnap, GreenJinn or CheckoutSmart. They'll show you all the items you can get for free or at a discount (such as 50p off). Then you purchase the items as normal and scan your receipt after you've shopped to get a rebate. It will load the money into your account on the app and when you've reached £10 you can then get it paid out via PayPal or into your bank account. You also get extra credit for referring friends.

☺ While printable coupons are not as popular as they used to be, you can still find them on websites, such as caringeveryday.co.uk. It's run by Johnson & Johnson and gives you money off their brands and is updated monthly.

☺ You can also find coupons in supermarket magazines, other magazines and newspapers and they'll often come with free samples. See the Free things chapter (pages 138–146) to find out more about how to get free stuff.

☺ You'll also find coupons on the products themselves, such as '50p off your next purchase'.

☺ Follow your favourite supermarkets or brands on social media as they'll often let you know about coupons, special offers or voucher codes. Make sure you follow the verified accounts — check they have a tick next to their name, so you know that it's not a scam account.

☺ If you're part of their loyalty scheme, stores will often send you coupons for certain products or vouchers to save money on your shopping.

☺ Check junk mail and inserts in local newspapers as you'll often find money-off vouchers for places, such as Farmfoods, within their promotional leaflets.

STOCKPILING – WHY I DO IT AND HOW YOU CAN TOO

I love stockpiling! I've been doing it for the past seven years, ever since I took my car in for a MOT and it came back needing a new gearbox that was going to cost an eye-watering £600. I knew I had to get my car fixed but I was worried about how I was going to afford my shopping that week. After that,

I decided that whenever I went shopping and saw a good offer, I was going to buy a few of the item on offer. That way I knew if I ever got another unexpected bill then I could go into my stockpile and I'd always have something to feed my family.

To most money savers, having a stockpile is a lifeline. It's a way of keeping things going when money is tighter than usual. It allows you that little bit of breathing space when cash isn't so readily available. Rather than worrying where your next box of washing powder is going to come from, it is already sat on the shelf waiting for you.

What is stockpiling?

Stockpiling isn't about hoarding things or clearing the shelves at the supermarket. It's about planning ahead and buying things that you know you're going to use. If you see a good offer on a product that you use regularly then buy one to use now and two for your stockpile. I stockpile things that I know my family goes through like cans of beans, soup, cereals and tomato ketchup. My kids go through loads of ketchup and if we ran out then we'd have to get it from the corner shop where the prices are higher. Instead, if I'm in Asda, then I'll pick up a few bottles, so I know there's some in my stockpile for when we run out. Try to stockpile ingredients you can make a meal out of — for me that's noodles, rice, pasta and cooking sauces. Once you start stockpiling, then you'll find you'll get into a position where you don't have to go shopping as regularly or buy as much when you do go shopping.

My stockpile

My stockpile takes up an entire wall of my garage and I organise it like the supermarket shelves. I put products into categories and organise them by date order. Items that need to be used up are near the front and things with a longer life are at the back. I have cleaning products and toiletries too and meat and other fresh produce is in my chest freezer.

I've either got all the items in my stockpile for cheap or for free. Over half of my stockpile includes gifts that I give to people for birthdays and Christmas. Every six months I have a sort out and donate anything I don't think I'm going to use to a charity or food bank, so nothing goes to waste. It even feeds my extended family too. My dad often comes round and fills a carrier bag with some cans from my stockpile.

How to start stockpiling

A lot of people think they don't have the space for a stockpile but start small. There are no rules about how big your stockpile needs to be, it's all about balance and finding out what works for you. Clear out a cupboard or find a space under a bed. Before I had my garage, I used a small shed in my garden.

The best way to start is to make a list of all the non-perishable items you use and go from there. Go to a bargain store and pick up your favourite brands that have good offers on — if it's a particularly good deal, and the product has a long shelf life, then double up and get six of each if you can afford to. I take Callum with me to Home Bargains when I'm buying jars and tins so he can help me carry them to the car. If I've got a few of them in it means I don't have to make the trip there every week, which also means I save money on petrol too.

Where do you find things for your stockpile?

One of the main ways is finding reduced-to-clear items and stocking up on them. You can also use coupons to get reduced items that can be added to your stockpile. However, both these ways aren't quick. It will take time to find reduced items and coupons are becoming harder to get hold of.

The foolproof way of starting your stockpile is to simply add a few extra of an item to your shopping when you can, using the 'buy one for now, two for later' rule. In a very short space of time this will build up a good stockpile.

Won't that mean I'm spending more money when I should be saving it?

In the beginning, yes, but you can't make a stockpile out of nothing, you need a little investment. However, after just a few weeks of buying now to use later, and only when items are on offer, you'll be amazed at the stockpile you've already created. It will then allow you to remove several items from your shopping list for the next few months, saving you money so you can spend it on something else.

Don't get hung up on how big your stockpile is either. It isn't the size that matters, it's how you use it.

Holly's **HACKS**

Savvy shopping hacks

If the online store that you're shopping from has **'live chat'**, why not jump on and ask for a discount? What have you got to lose?

If you have a favourite shop that you know you'll buy from regularly, **sign up each adult member of your household to their newsletter** so you'll have multiple discount codes to use when you shop there.

EXPERT HACKS!

Thanks to **Iwan** at **mrcarrington.co.uk** for the following two excellent hacks!

When you're looking for furniture for your home, consider buying second hand, or even better, getting stuff for free. Websites like freecycle, Gumtree and eBay will often have really good-quality pieces at a fraction of the price of the shops or the British Heart Foundation has some fantastic deals. It's worth checking Facebook Marketplace too as often you can pick up great bargains from people selling in your local area.

When you're at the garden centre, look for plant pots with a chip in them. They may discount them for you at the checkout and you can simply turn the pot around so that the chip isn't on show.

AMAZING MEMBERS' HACKS

'If you buy a lot of stamps, the Royal Mail usually announces when stamp prices are going to increase. I always make sure I stock up before the price goes up as I run a small business and it saves me a lot of money.'

'Check if your work has a benefits scheme that will give you discounts in shops and supermarkets. My workplace has Perkbox and I never used to check it. But now I use it all the time and have saved hundreds of pounds.'

'Sign-up to Airtime Rewards and earn money towards your mobile phone bill when you shop (you link your debit and credit cards and it tracks your purchases). It's a great way to earn money for shopping in stores, such as Primark which aren't on cashback websites. You can also earn money for referring your friends.'

Amazon bargain hunting

When it comes to buying online, Amazon is a one-stop shop that has it all. I love Amazon and I'm on it every single day looking for bargains to share with my followers. But it's a complex site that can be hard to navigate for some people. There are sections that many people don't even know exist. But if you learn how to find your way around it, as well as knowing quick ways to search it, there are some great deals to be had. Here's how to save yourself money and find some of the best bargains.

Amazon Prime

If you shop on Amazon regularly it's worth getting Amazon Prime. As well as free next day delivery for a year and getting priority to the sales, you also get access to Amazon's version of Netflix. It allows you to watch exclusive Amazon original movies and series as well as popular movies and TV shows.

How to qualify for free delivery if you don't have Prime

If you don't have Amazon prime, unless you spend over £20 then you'll have to pay for delivery. This can be VERY frustrating especially if the item you're buying is £18.99! Luckily there's a website called fillerchecker.co.uk where you enter the amount you need to spend to qualify for free delivery and it will search Amazon for items in that price range. At the time of writing, the £20 minimum spend for free delivery applies to all items other than books. With books you get free delivery if the amount is £10 or over.

Find the bargains with an Amazon discount finder

There are many Amazon discount finder websites which give you a quick way to find the bargains. My favourite is jungle-search.com (make sure you select the UK as your location). All you have to do is select the category you want to search in and the discount level (up to 95%) and it will search the entire site and show you the best deals. If you're looking for something more targeted, you can add a keyword, such as 'Disney', and it will give you results for items in that brand. This is a great way to find discounted toys for Christmas and birthday presents.

Subscribe and save

If you're buying items from Amazon regularly, you'll save money if you use 'subscribe and save'. It's a subscription service available for thousands of products, just choose the item and how often you want it delivered and you'll get 5% off and free delivery.

I use Amazon to bulk buy household products like toilet bleach, dishwasher tablets and loo rolls for my stockpile. It saves you a trip to the supermarket and it means bulky items are delivered straight to your door, so you don't have to carry them home. If you only want to buy something once and get the discount, then order it and immediately cancel any future deliveries.

Use price drop tracking websites

Websites such as uk.camelcamelcamel.com track price drops on Amazon. They're definitely worth checking before you place an order, especially if you're buying an expensive product.

Check out the daily deals

Every day Amazon has 'daily deals' with selected products from each category which you'll find in the 'Today's deals' section of the site. The average saving is around 30% but it can be as high as 70%. Some of these items are called 'lightning deals', which means there are a selected number of products available for that price before it goes back to its retail price. It's basically first come, first served with these so be quick. They're extremely popular on Prime day, which are days in the year that have exclusive offers for Prime members, and you can get some fantastic deals. Last year I got some Philips Smart Lights for £50 that were normally over £100 each.

Amazon vouchers

Most people don't know that Amazon has a voucher page where you can find discount codes for popular products. Click on the item to collect the voucher for that product, then if you choose to buy it, the voucher will automatically be applied at the checkout. It's updated regularly, so the discounts change.

Amazon Warehouse

Amazon Warehouse re-sells millions of like-new, pre-owned items that have been returned by customers at a discounted price.

Amazon Outlet

This is a little-known section of the site where you can get discounts on overstocked or clearance items.

Save money by topping up your account

Occasionally Amazon will have 'top-up' promotions where you can save money by topping up your Amazon account. So, for example if you top up your Amazon account by £60 then you'll get £6 free. The balance sits in your account until you make a purchase and it's similar to a gift card.

Buy directly from Amazon

When you search for items on Amazon it won't only show items sold by Amazon itself but also items sold by third-party sellers via Amazon Marketplace. When you buy something from Amazon Marketplace the prices are often marked up as the seller has to pay Amazon fees. Also, if you're not happy with your item you'll need to organise your return with the seller directly and sometimes this can be problematic. Marketplace purchases are covered by Amazon's protection guarantee but I prefer to buy directly from Amazon.

Check out the movers and shakers

The Amazon Movers and Shakers page shows Amazon's top-selling products for the last twenty-four hours. Top-selling items may be due to popularity (such as a new-release games console) or due to a high discount. It's always worth checking this page as it's a good way of alerting you to items that are being snapped up because they're a really good bargain. You can also search it by category and it's a great way to find cheap toys for birthdays and Christmas.

Amazon hacks

If you're a **student**, you can get a six-month trial for Amazon Prime for free. After your free trial you get the discounted rate per month. (Amazon also offers a 30-day free trial for non-students.) So, if you don't use Amazon regularly but want to take advantage of Prime services for a month, you can sign-up and then cancel it before your trial renews.

Discount finder websites are a good way to spot price glitches. I once got a hundred dishwasher tablets for £5 and members of my Facebook group have even picked up a £799 laptop for £50. Amazon send things out so quickly that sometimes by the time the glitch has been discovered, the items have already been delivered so the majority of the time they have to honour it. Always try to spot glitches but never assume you're going to get the item at that price until it's in your hand.

AMAZING MEMBERS' HACKS

'If you see something you like being sold by an Amazon Marketplace seller, Google their company. Prices will more than likely be cheaper on their own website as they don't have to pay fees to Amazon.'

'Download the Vipon app. It has coupon codes for selected Amazon products where you can save at least 50%.'

'Put things in your basket and leave them there, that way you'll get a notification when the price has decreased. I saved £100 on a Shark vacuum cleaner doing this.'

'If you have an Amazon Prime account, sometimes you can choose no rush delivery instead of next day delivery. You'll get a reward from Amazon for doing so (such as credit to use against your next purchase).'

'You can share Amazon Prime benefits with one other adult and children by forming an Amazon "household".'

Clothing, beauty and make-up savings

I never pay full price for make-up and clothes. Whether you're shopping online or in store, there are always so many offers and deals available and ways that you can save.

SAVING MONEY ON CLOTHES

If you're on a budget, buying clothes is often a luxury that you can't afford. But with a bit of shopping around and finding the best deals and discounts, you need never pay full price again.

Look for online discount codes

When you're shopping online, if you know you want to buy a particular item of clothing, always make sure that you check the homepage of the website to see if there's a discount code. Websites such as PrettyLittleThing rotate their coupon codes every twenty-four hours. So, if it's free delivery one day, it's likely to be a discount the next day. Depending on what you're buying and how much it costs, work out which will save you the most money and wait for that offer.

Avoiding delivery charges

If you shop regularly on fashion websites such as ASOS it's worth paying the set price for one year's free delivery. You can also add items to your basket to get free delivery if it works out cheaper. For example, if a clothing website has free delivery when you spend over £40 but your total is £39, search the site from 'low to high' to find something small like a pair of socks which will make up the price difference.

Keep an eye on sales

If you buy something online and it goes on sale a few days later, you can always return it and buy it at the cheaper price. But if you've already taken the tags off and worn it, then drop the company an email expressing your disappointment. They'll sometimes refund the difference or give you a discount on your next purchase to make sure that you continue to shop with them. This happened to me recently with a rainbow top that I bought online. Two days after I'd got it, it went on sale and I was so annoyed as I'd already worn it and removed the tags. I went onto their live chat and told them what had happened, and they refunded the £5 difference. It's good customer service and they want to keep you happy so it's definitely worth asking.

Don't rush to buy

You can save money on high-street clothing on websites like everything5pounds.com which sells ex-high street stock for only £5. They regularly have items on offer for £2.50 too.

If you're not in a rush to buy an item, add it to your cart on the website and leave it there for a few days. Some retailers will email you saying, 'have you forgotten something?'. Within this email they'll sometimes try to entice you to complete your purchase by sending you a discount code.

How to avoid fast fashion

Upcycle your old clothes instead. If you've got a plain T-shirt that you're a bit bored with then give it a new lease of life. Have a look on YouTube for some ideas about how to cut a T-shirt into a different shape or buy some iron-on transfers. Or why not tie-dye it? Tie-dye is so fashionable right now and you can buy simple kits online. My kids love doing this.

Go for a trawl around charity shops. I'm lucky enough to have some amazing charity stores near me. They sort out the clothes rails into colours, so it's easy to put an outfit together. I recently picked up a Monsoon top for £1.50.

Check out second-hand selling sites and apps. I like Depop because you can see people wearing the clothes that they're selling, and a lot of influencers and YouTubers sell their stuff on there. When you see something you like, you message the seller and you can negotiate, especially if it's been on there for a while. You can also search for different types of clothing.

Saving when you're shopping in store

Check the stitching, hem and buttons on any item that you're buying. Even if there's a minor fault like a pull or a few stitches missing, you can ask for some money off and repair it yourself at home.

Buy from the men's section. Casual clothes like basic jumpers, T-shirts, sweatshirts and hoodies are often much cheaper if you buy them in the smaller sizes from the men's section.

Before you snap up any bargains, read the label for care instructions and avoid anything that's dry clean only, which will cost you more money down the line to look after.

EXPERT HACKS FOR CHARITY SHOPPING!

My friend, Youtuber **Kate McCabe (@Katemccabey** on Instagram) is a bargain hunter and charity shop queen. These are her top six tips for getting the best out of charity shopping.

Take your time

You can be lucky and find treasure in the first charity shop you visit but more often than not you'll need to spend a couple of hours looking for bargains. Be patient — you will find them.

Have a good rummage

Have a good look in the shelves, boxes of items, clearance sections and look underneath things as the bargains might be hidden.

Don't dither

If you see something that you like, don't hang about. If you leave it behind, chances are it will be gone when you come back.

Look through all the clothes

A lot of people say they can't find much in their charity shops and this often comes down to looking. Always look at different sizes of clothes because they all vary, and vintage clothes usually come up smaller. It's worth having a proper look through the rails as items are sometimes put in the wrong places so you might miss out on a gem.

Check out the homeware

Don't forget to look in the homeware sections. I've found so much treasure for my house second hand. Many people donate unwanted gifts so you can also find lots of brand-new items.

Give as well as receive

Take some donations when you go charity shopping, so you create space in your house for new purchases as well as help the charity shop.

Why some designer outlets might not be the bargain they seem

Have you ever been to an outlet shopping centre and thought that you were getting a bargain? The merchandise on sale in some of these stores isn't always outdated seasonal products from their retail stores. Many brands make cheaper quality clothes exclusively to be sold in their outlet stores.

In the US, it's thought that 65—80% of stock in the outlet stores is made especially for them but how can you tell? If there's a designer item that you really want, then look at it carefully first in the retail store then you can compare it to the product that you see at the outlet. With purses and bags, look at the quality of the leather, the stitching and also the logo. Often with clothes you can spot the differences in the quality of the fabrics. If you want a genuine designer bag or item of clothing, then it might be worth saving up for the real deal rather than buying an inferior product from an outlet.

BARGAIN BEAUTY AND MAKE-UP

There's nothing I love more than a good pampering session, and you can still treat yourself even if you're on a budget. Read on to find out how I do it.

Ask for free samples

You can ask for free samples of high-end make-up and skincare online and only pay for the postage — www. feelunique.com will also refund you the £3.95 postage if you go on to purchase the full-sized item. This is great for buying foundation online so you can get the right shade and also for trying out high-end skincare ranges.

If you're buying perfume, see if there's a gift set available as sometimes you get more in a gift set than buying the perfume on its own. I recently wanted to buy a J-Lo perfume and it was £50 to buy 100ml but there was a 100ml gift set for £25 that also came with a body lotion and a miniature fragrance.

Ask for free samples in department stores and at perfume counters too. I've also found Lush are particularly good at giving free samples if you ask to try some of their products.

Most stores will let you return make-up and skincare if you find it doesn't suit your skin type. Boots No7 is really good for this.

Treasures in the clearance section

Always check the clearance section in stores, such as Boots and Superdrug, for beauty bargains. I've found some amazing bargains in Boots including a £100 Slendertone for £20 and a £60 hairdryer for a fiver. It's completely random what's in them and it varies from store to store but it's always worth a look.

Buy discounted high-end make-up like MAC and Anastasia Beverly Hills at TK Maxx and the original factory shop. You'll be buying products that are out of season but with make-up it doesn't really matter and you're getting expensive products for a fraction of the cost.

You can often find discontinued Rimmel, Max Factor, Maybelline and Barry M products in Poundland. You can pick up some amazing bargains like two nail varnishes or eyeshadows for £1.

Look for loyalty schemes

Check loyalty scheme apps, such as Boots Advantage Card and Superdrug Beautycard, for discounts on beauty products.

Try before you buy

You can book a free makeover at certain beauty counters, such as Boots No7 and Benefit, where a professional make-up artist will apply your make-up. It's a great way to get free expert advice on products. At other counters you have to pay for a makeover but it's redeemable against purchases. So, if you know you're going to buy something from Charlotte Tilbury for example, it's worth getting a makeover thrown in.

Supermarket skincare savings

Budget supermarkets can be great for affordable skincare too. Some anti-ageing creams sold in Aldi and Lidl are comparable to high-end brands in tests and they're made to be 'dupes'.

One thing I would advise is, don't waste money on cheap make-up brushes. I've found that if you buy cheap, you have to buy often as the bristles drop out. Invest in quality brands like Spectrum in Black Friday sales or at Christmas when you'll often get a whole set for a discounted price.

HOW TO SAVE ON HAIRDRESSERS AND BEAUTY TREATMENTS

☺ Use Groupon and Wowcher to find reduced deals at hair and beauty salons near you. Local businesses use these websites to advertise their promotions and get you through the door in the hope that you'll be a return customer.

☺ Go to a beauty college to get your hair done or have a treatment. I get a wash and a blow-dry for £1.50 at my local college and it's only £7.50 for highlights. I've always had a great experience and they've got their trainers watching them. They're priced according to what level of training they're at — level three students are in their final year.

☺ Local hair salons are always looking for models for their trainees to practise on. They'll often have a training day once a week in their salon. Blow-drys and haircuts are normally free, and colour treatments are a reduced price.

☺ Some big-name spas, such as Bannatyne's, have spa days for sale on Wowcher for a large discount. Callum and I got a £307 spa day for two people with lunch, products and treatments for £119.

Holly's HACKS

Beauty hacks

Always ask for a freebie. If you're ordering something online from a make-up or beauty company, it's always worth asking if they've got any freebies that they could send you. I did this when I ordered something from Lush. In the 'any additional notes' box I wrote *I love freebies so if you have any please include them!* When my order arrived, it came with loads of samples of soap and five different shampoos. Always add a little thank you or a friendly comment to your online order. You never know, you might get some free samples in return for being friendly.

If you're a student you can get a **student discount** at many retailers such as French Connection, River Island and ASOS. It's normally 10% but look out for the occasional 20% offers around September.

EXPERT BEAUTY HACKS!

My friend and professional make-up artist, **Amy Coombes** (**@amycoombess** on Instagram), has shared her top beauty hacks with us.

Try before you buy

If there's a product that you've been eyeing up for a few months but you're not a fan of the price tag, ask for a sample. Most counters will be happy to provide them and they're not always as small as you might think.

Customise your make-up

One of my fave hacks is to mix eyeshadows with concealer to create eyeliner in any shade and finish that you like without having to spend the £££.

RIP THE SPONGE OFF!

If you have a concealer or a foundation that has a sponge applicator where you have to twist the tube in order for the product to come out, rip that sponge off. You'll get so much more product out of the tube.

Get a free lipstick

Back to MAC is a great way to treat yourself to a free lipstick. Just return six empty MAC products and in return you'll receive a lipstick of your choice.

Look for dupes

If there's a product you've been wanting that is a little more on the luxury or expensive side, my fave thing to do before taking the plunge is to google a 'drugstore dupe' and see what's available.

For Spring

Spring to me is all about crafts, eating chocolate and getting out and about in the fresh air. You can do all of that and more with these simple step-by-step creations.

SALT DOUGH

This is similar to the Homemade Play-Doh (in Autumn section) but can be used to make little decorations and ornaments, which are then baked so that they last for years.

You will need

Baking sheet

Greaseproof baking paper

250g plain flour, plus extra for dusting

125g table salt

A large bowl

125ml water

Chopping board

Different shaped biscuit cutters (optional)

Kebab skewer or pencil (optional)

Paint

Paintbrush

Ribbon or string (optional)

How to do it

1. Preheat your oven to low — around 80°C (60°C fan) will do — and line a baking sheet with greaseproof baking paper.

2. Mix the flour and table salt together in a large bowl, then add the water and stir until the dough starts to come together in a soft ball.

3. Take a chopping board and dust it lightly with flour, transfer your dough to the board and start to shape your designs. You could make little chicks or Easter eggs. You can use different shaped biscuit cutters to do this, or my girls like to make them into shapes themselves.

4. If you're intending to hang your decorations, use a kebab skewer or pencil to pierce a small hole about 1cm from the edge of the top of your shape.

5. Spread your decorations evenly on your lined baking sheet and bake for 3 hours until they've hardened.

6. Leave to cool for at least an hour and then paint or decorate as you wish. Thread some ribbon or string through them if you like and use them as Easter decorations or hide them as little extra treats as part of your egg hunt.

HOMEMADE PIÑATA-STYLE GIANT EGGS

These giant eggs are an instant hit with any child. They take very little effort to make and they're great for Easter. Put chocolate eggs inside them or toys from Poundland and then on Easter Sunday, rip them open. They work well for birthday parties too. Everyone will cheer when the egg breaks and reveals its contents.

You will need
A large mixing bowl
Plain flour
Water
Scissors
Old newspaper
A balloon
Paintbrushes
Old mug or empty glass jar
Paint
Filler items, such as sweets, toy cars, dolls
String (optional)

How to do it

1. Get a mixing bowl and add equal measures of plain flour and water. Mix to make a paste.
2. Cut up scraps of newspaper to make the papier-mâché pieces.
3. Blow up the balloon and then start pasting the paper strips onto it with the glue mix. Make sure you leave a small gap, big enough to fit your filler items through. If you plan on hanging up your giant egg, create a small handle at the top so you can tie some string to it.
4. When you've completely covered the balloon, add a second layer to strengthen the shell. Each additional layer you add will make it stronger and harder to break.
5. Leave it to dry overnight by balancing it on top of an old mug or empty glass jar.
6. When the shell has dried and it's solid, pop the balloon with your scissors and start painting the outside with whatever design you like. You could decorate it like a giant Easter egg, for example.
7. Balance the egg back on the mug or jar and leave to dry for several hours.
8. Once the paint has dried, add your filler items to the egg and then cover the hole with more paper and paste. Leave to dry before decorating to blend in with the rest of the egg.
9. The egg can then be hung up, but I prefer to let the children rip it open to reveal the treats inside.

BUTTERFLY GOODIE BAGS

These butterfly bags are practically ZERO effort but look so sweet. I like to use them as bonus finds during Easter egg hunts as you can fill them with slightly healthier treats like raisins, dried bananas and nuts.

You will need
Clothes pegs
Felt-tip pens (optional)
Pipe cleaners
Scissors
Clear resealable sandwich bags
Googly eyes
Glue (optional)
Snacks of your choice

How to do it
1. Get a handful of plain clothes pegs and, if you like, decorate them with felt-tip pens. You can also leave them plain.
2. Trim your pipe cleaners to about 7.5cm long and curl the ends into a spiral shape. These will be your butterfly antennae.
3. Pop a couple of googly eyes on the peg to give your butterfly a face. They usually have a sticky pad on the back of them but if they don't you'll need to glue them in place.
4. Half fill each sandwich bag with the treats of your choice and seal them up. Make sure they're only half full as you're going to need to push the contents to the side to make room for your pegs.
5. Squeeze the bags in the middle and attach one clothes peg to each one. Hide or place them around your house or garden to be found by your scavengers.

HOME-GROWN CRESS EGG HEADS

These egg heads are a brilliant way to get your little ones into planting and growing things and they look really fun. Once they've grown, you can use them to make a tasty egg and cress sandwich too.

You will need

Hard-boiled eggs, cooled
Felt-tip pens
Googly eyes
Glue (optional)
Cotton wool
Cress seeds
An egg carton
Scissors

How to do it

1. Get a cooled hard-boiled egg and draw a face on it with your felt-tips then stick on a pair of googly eyes. They usually have a sticky pad on the back of them but if they don't you'll need to glue them in place.

2. Chop off the top of the egg and remove the egg from the shell, trying to keep the shell as intact as possible. This is slightly tricky but don't worry if you crack the shell too much.

3. Gently stuff some cotton wool into your hollowed out eggshell and sprinkle a dozen or so cress seeds inside.

4. Place the eggs back in the egg carton and then lightly water the seeds and place on a windowsill. Follow the instructions on the seed packet to take the best care of your cress.

5. After about a week, the seeds should have sprouted and started to grow. When the shoots have grown their leaves they're ready to harvest.

6. Grab some scissors, snip away and enjoy your home-grown cress.

STICKY SCAVENGER HUNT

This is a great outdoor activity to get your children into the fresh air. You can do this one several times as each location you visit will be a new challenge. Why not combine this activity with the butterfly bags (see previous pages) to reward them as they go?.

You will need
A piece of cardboard
Ruler
Marker pen
A selection of natural treasures, such as leaves, flowers, seeds, pine cones, stones and twigs
Double-sided sticky tape

How to do it
1. Take your cardboard and mark out the title section and columns and rows.

2. Go to the destination before your walk and pick a small selection of leaves, flowers or shrubs that are easily found there, such as acorns, dandelions or twigs.

3. Stick the items to the board with your tape.

4. Take your board on a walk with the family and let your kids spot the items attached, ticking them off or sticking them in when they find them.

AMAZING MEMBERS' HACKS

'If you take a bag of old clothing to H&M, they will give you a voucher for £5 off your next purchase of £25 or more.'

'Buy at the end of each season to save a fortune on clothes. Every September I go to Asda and pick up clothes for as little as 50p for the following summer (just don't forget to size-up for your kids!).'

'If you're buying clothes online from a company that has a retail store, such as New Look, opt for 'Click and Collect' to save on delivery costs. It's handy if you haven't reached the free delivery threshold.'

'If you find a seller on Depop with lots of items you like, ask them if they will list them as a bundle for a lower price.'

'Save money on hairspray and use tumble dryer sheets to tame flyaway hairs instead. They work a treat.'

'Save spending cash on expensive spot treatments and use egg whites instead. Apply one whipped egg white to your face, leave it on until it dries and then wipe it off. It makes a great face mask for oily or spotty skin.'

Shopping for babies and kids

I've always been into money saving so as soon as I found out I was pregnant with my daughter, Mollie, nine years ago, and then Bella nine months later, I was straight on it trying to win competitions and get coupons and freebies from brands. Babies are expensive, but the brands want your business because they know you're likely to stick with them while your baby is small, so there are lots of freebies and discounts to be had. Even if you want that expensive travel system, there are ways to get it cheaper than you think.

Join in-store baby clubs

One of my favourites is Boots Parenting Club. As soon as you sign up, you get a freebie for joining and it's normally really nice stuff like a changing bag or a baby toiletry set. You also get vouchers and promotions from baby brands and extra Advantage Card points. There's also the Asda Baby & Toddler Club which offers free advice, offers, promotions and competitions.

Join an online parenting club for free packs

The two most popular ones are Emma's Diary and Bounty. With Emma's Diary you can get three free packs throughout your pregnancy — mum-to-be, bump-to-baby and new family — that contain branded products and samples. You collect them from either Boots or Argos and when you sign up you also get access to an app and week-by-week updates throughout your pregnancy. Bounty also offer three free packs — a pregnancy information pack which you get from your midwife, a mum-to-be pack that you can collect from Boots, Asda or Tesco and a newborn pack which you're given at the hospital after your baby's birth. You have to download the app to get them, which also gives you updates about your baby's development.

These online clubs are worth joining as the free packs contain lots of handy samples from nappy cream, wipes and nappies to breast pads, stretch mark cream and washing powder. It's always a surprise what you're going to get in them and there are often little treats in there for you too like a nice bar of chocolate, a soft drink sample or a body cream. But what I would say is these schemes are designed to collect your data. When you sign up, they will ask for your email address, postal address and sometimes a phone number. If you already have a secondary email set up for loyalty schemes, newsletters and vouchers then give that them one or set up one specifically for your pregnancy as you'll be bombarded with emails. Don't give your phone number. I made that mistake and I was hounded with phone calls from companies trying to sell me life insurance. By the time I was pregnant with Bella, I'd learnt my lesson so I either crossed out the phone number box or gave them a fake one. I didn't mind them having my address as they'll send you offers and coupons related to your baby's age, such as teething and weaning products.

Clubs run by food and formula brands

When you sign up to the Cow & Gate baby club, they often send welcome gifts like a cute cuddly cow and a useful book about your baby's development. When your baby's six months old they'll send you coupons, samples and weaning advice.

When signing up to Ella's Kitchen Friends, they often send you a free weaning pack that includes wall charts and stickers, a coupon for money off one of their pouches and access to a weaning app.

Aptaclub run by Aptamil provides access to expert advice, offers and how-to guides for new club members. With SMA Baby Club you get a welcome pack, free advice and offers.

These baby clubs are definitely worth joining as some of them run a competition for everyone who has newly signed up (you have to prove that you're pregnant before you can claim your prize). I was well chuffed when I won £500 of John Lewis vouchers when I was pregnant with Cloud.

HOW TO SAVE MONEY ON NAPPIES

Nappies are a major expense so it's worth writing to baby brands asking for free samples because they really want you to use their products. Just before I had Cloud, I wrote to every single nappy brand from the disposable ones to the organic and the reusable brands, politely asking them if they had any samples or coupons because my baby was due in a month and I wanted to try their brand. I received so many that I had the first month's supply of nappies for Cloud completely free and I still had loads left which I donated to a food bank.

Bulk buy online

If you're pregnant or you have children, it's worth joining Amazon Family. You enter your baby's due date or your children's dates of birth and you'll receive personalised product recommendations based on your child's age and discounts for these products. If you're a Prime member, you'll also get up to 20% off nappies and baby food when you order them via the subscribe and save programme. This is a great way to bulk buy nappies. You get free next day delivery

and they deliver them straight to your door. Huggies®
nappies were brilliant for my girls, but they don't make them
any more, and the only ones to keep Cloud dry are Pampers,
so I get them whenever they're on offer at Amazon and bulk
buy them.

Get the best deals

To find the best price for nappies use Bumdeal.co.uk. It
compares the prices of all nappies, works out the price
per nappy and tells you where you can get them cheapest.
You search according to brand and size and it also includes
baby wipes.

BUYING BABY CLOTHES AND EQUIPMENT

Like I did with the nappies, when I was heavily pregnant
with Cloud, I sent out cards to around thirty brands. I
explained that I was interested in trying out their products
to use with my baby and asked if they had any coupons or
free samples available. I had so many things sent to me
including bottles, baby wipes and a huge set of dummies
worth £20. If you're pregnant, then why not give it a try and
reach out to a brand that you like the look of. For new brands
especially, positive reviews are so valuable to them and every
brand wants you to become a long-term customer.

Shop at supermarket baby events

Supermarkets like Asda, Tesco and Lidl all have week-long
baby and toddler events several times a year. They're worth
a look as they have some cracking offers and bulk buys and
are a great way to save a lot of money.

But my top tip is to wait for the week after the baby events
have finished as it can be an even better time to find a

bargain. The stores will buy things in bulk for these events and afterwards they need to get rid of any leftover stock. I've picked up baby gates and car seats for only a fiver like this. If you're only just pregnant, then don't buy at the baby events but wait and see if anything is reduced afterwards.

Buy second hand

Car boot sales are a really good place to find newborn baby clothes. People tend to sell them in bundles. Most babies are only in that size for a few weeks so they're usually in immaculate condition. My children have all been small when they were born so I've always bought tiny baby bundles from car boots. I once got ten Next sleepsuits for £1.

Prams, pushchairs, cots and Moses baskets are all good to buy second hand but always make sure that you buy a new mattress. I would not advise buying a second-hand car seat as you don't know if it's been in an accident and any damage might not be visible.

Get a trade discount at baby shows

I went to the Baby Show when I was thirty-six weeks pregnant with Cloud. I still didn't have a travel system and I couldn't find anything second hand. All the brands were there like iCandy, Bugaboo and Cosatto and you could try out all the prams and even push them around a track. You can also take advantage of trade promotions. I got a Cosatto travel system for £350 that retails for £1,200. I couldn't even buy it second hand for that price.

The largest baby show in the UK is the Baby Show which takes place three times a year in different locations including

London and Birmingham. They have great goody bags that you can buy for £5 but contain £30 worth of stuff and you can buy as many of them as you want. You also get lots of samples and freebies from the brands. I haven't needed to buy any nappy cream since I went to the show as I got so many samples. There are also smaller local shows, but the deals aren't as good. It's worth travelling to one of the bigger shows as you can save a lot of money.

Join bargain groups on Facebook

Alongside my Facebook group Extreme Couponing and Bargains, I also run Baby and Toddler Deals UK, which has more than 40,000 members. It's a place where people can share bargains, but they can also share helpful advice and recommendations.

Make an Amazon Baby wishlist for newborn essentials

When you have a baby or have a baby shower, people kindly want to buy you things, but chances are you'll get stuff that you won't really use or that you've already bought. Plus lots of newborn clothes that your baby probably won't even get the chance to wear. I hate to think of people wasting their money so instead, set up an Amazon wishlist so if people want to give you a gift, they can choose something they know that you really want or will use. Make sure there are lots of little items on there and that the prices cover all budgets. People don't have to buy off your list, but it gives them suggestions.

FREE CHILDREN'S MEDICATION

In some areas of the UK you can get free medication for kids, including pricey head lice treatment, as part of the NHS's

Minor Ailments Scheme. But please don't abuse this service — it's not a way of stocking up on free medication. It's a way of getting help if your child is ill and you're really struggling. You can buy generic non-branded paracetamol for as little as £1.

Family shopping hacks

Cashback for your kids. When you're shopping online, use a cashback website, such as KidStart. Instead of the commission you earn on your shopping being paid to you, it goes into a bank account for your child which they can access when they're eighteen.

Collect your **Bounty bags from Asda** if you can. I collected mine from different places and found the one from Asda had a lot more of their own products in it. There was a whole pack of newborn nappies and a pack of sleepsuits. The other bags I collected were just filled with leaflets and a few samples.

If you're buying **prenatal vitamins** don't go for the ones branded especially for pregnancy. The ingredients are often the same as ordinary multivitamins, you're just paying £3 or £4 more for the ones specifically marketed at pregnant women. Zinc supplements are the same. I found basic zinc tablets on sale for 49p, but the ones marketed at pregnant women were £2.49.

AMAZING MEMBERS' HACKS

'Pillowcases make ideal Moses basket mattress sheets in an emergency.'

'To quickly get wet sand off your kids at the beach, sprinkle them with talc. It absorbs the water and the sand brushes straight off. No more sandy feet.'

'When your child grows out of their cot, take one side off and turn it into a desk.'

'Pool noodles make great bed guards for kids.'

'A muffin case threaded through the bottom of an ice-lolly stick is great for catching drips.'

'If you're on benefits and having a baby, you can get a one-off payment of £500 to help towards the cost of having a child. It's called the Sure Start Maternity Grant and you'll qualify if you're having your first child or already have a child but are expecting a multiple birth.'

'Try reusable nappies. I never thought I'd like them but now I'd never go back to disposables.'

'If you're pregnant or have a child under four and you're on means-tested benefits, you can get "Healthy Start vouchers". These are worth £3.10 every week and can be spent on milk, fresh and frozen fruit and vegetables and infant formula milk. You can also get free vitamins.'

'Buy gender-neutral baby clothes and accessories if you plan on having another baby. This saved me £100s when I fell pregnant with my little boy as I didn't need to rush out and buy anything new.'

'If you're pregnant or have had a baby in the last twelve months you can get free NHS prescriptions and dental treatment. All you have to do is show proof, such as your maternity exemption certificate.'

How to save hundreds of pounds on your bills

When it comes to bills, a lot of people just switch off. Ultimately, it's easier not to think about it. But getting your bills sorted is an easy way to instantly save yourself hundreds of pounds and it will feel so good when you do it. Even if you just take half an hour out of your day to look through your bills and direct debits, it will be worth it as there's so much money to be saved. Follow my easy guide to find the simple things that you can do today to slash the cost of your household bills.

• •

SWITCH TO THE BEST TARIFF

When you move into a new home, the energy provider that the previous residents had will automatically put you on to their standard tariff, which is often the most expensive one.

Perhaps you've been on the same tariff with the same company for years? If so, chances are you're probably paying way over the odds. Energy companies know that most people go for convenience and they can take advantage of that. If you don't want the hassle of having to change your energy company, then make sure that you're on the best possible rate with your current provider and not the standard tariff. They're normally very competitive and want to keep you as a customer so contact them and ask them what's the best deal that they can give you.

But if you really want to save money then it could be worth switching to a different provider. You're looking at saving between £300 and £600 per year by doing this and it's something that I do every twelve months.

Use a price comparison website

If you're going to switch provider, then use a price comparison website to help you shop around and compare rates. But when you're using these websites always make sure that your search includes 'all providers' (sometimes you have to tick a box when you search) as sometimes they might only recommend the ones that they make a commission from.

Once you've worked out the provider with the best tariff for you, don't buy it through the price comparison website. Go on to a cashback website, such as Quidco or TopCashback, and you'll get a lump sum for switching. Every time I change my provider, I get around £100 cashback so it's easy money. Just use the price comparison website as a research tool.

Get a water meter

Unlike electricity providers, you can't change your water supplier but if you can, get a water meter. That way you'll only pay for the water that you use rather than the standard rate. I used to live in a flat where I couldn't get a water meter. I had a fixed rate water bill of around £90 every month and at times I really struggled to pay it. Then I moved into my first house where I could get a meter and my bills went down to a more manageable £30.

Use a smart meter

A smart meter will make you more conscious of how much energy you're using and will help you change your habits. You'll see how much energy you can save by doing small things like turning your thermostat down a couple of degrees or having a shorter shower. It definitely makes you more mindful of your household spending. You can get them for free from your electricity provider or you can buy them.

Wash your clothes on cold

The cooler your washing machine, the more money you're going to save. If your clothes aren't massively stained or dirty, then try washing them on a cold wash. It still gets them clean and it also helps them to last longer.

Get money back for washing your uniform

If you have to wear a uniform for work, then did you know that you can get the money back for the cost of washing it at home? It's called the Uniform Tax Rebate and the amount you get back can be backdated and can range from anything from £60 to £150 or more per year. There are websites that will make the claim for you, but they'll take a percentage of the payment so go straight to the government website and fill out the form yourself. It takes minutes and the rebate covers any kind of uniform from a branded T-shirt to a full uniform and can be claimed each year.

Buy an Eco Egg

Instead of using washing powder or expensive liquitabs, try an Eco Egg. It's a little plastic egg that comes with pellets that you put inside it. One egg costs around £12 on Amazon and the pellets last for 210 washes so it will save you a lot of money and it works well. I've used one to wash Cloud's sick-covered baby clothes and they've come out fine! It's great for people with allergies and you can choose from different natural scents if you're missing that washing powder smell.

CHECK IF YOU NEED A TV LICENCE

A TV licence costs £157.50 a year but many people don't realise that they don't actually need one. You only need a licence if you:

- ◎ Watch or record programmes as they're being shown live on TV on any channel.
- ◎ Watch or stream programmes live on an online TV service (such as ITV Hub, All 4, YouTube, Amazon Prime Video, NOW TV, Sky Go, etc.)
- ◎ Download or watch any BBC programmes on iPlayer.

If you're a student then you don't need a TV licence if your parents have one at your home address and the device that you're watching TV on, such as an iPhone, laptop or tablet, isn't plugged in at the time of watching.

GET ON TOP OF YOUR DIRECT DEBITS

Have a good look at your bank account and double check what's coming out of your account each month. You'd be surprised at how many people have old direct debits that they've forgotten to cancel. A common one is paying for pet insurance after your pet has died. Some people only realise when the renewal letter comes through. It's always worth having a look at your direct debits every few months and asking yourself — do I really need this? Am I actually using it? Or can I haggle on it?

I see so many people with gym memberships they're not using or magazine subscriptions for magazines that they never read who would be better off cancelling them. Always check your bank account as errors can be made. You might get charged twice or realise one of your direct debits has gone up, so you need to contact the company and find out why. Be on top of things and be aware.

SAVE BY SKIMMING

Skimming is when you round up your purchases to the nearest whole number and the extra goes into a savings account. So, if you buy something in a shop for £2.80 then some app-based banks like Monzo and Starling will round your purchase up to £3 and the extra 20p will go into a different account. Sometimes it's only a penny or two but it's amazing how it adds up over time.

HELP IF YOU'RE STRUGGLING

If you're really struggling with your bills, the Energy Saving Trust offers free help and support (energysavingtrust.org. uk). They can advise you on all the grants and discounts available and can put you in touch with other organisations and charities that can help.

HOW TO SAVE ON YOUR BROADBAND AND TV

Make sure you haggle. A lot of people have Sky TV or Virgin and they just leave it running after their contract runs out. Don't do it! If it's due for renewal, you're in a prime position and now is your time to haggle. Ring up your provider and see what they can offer you to stay as well as contacting other companies to see if you can get a better deal.

Always go through to the cancellation line. If you're switching broadband or TV provider, then always ask to be put through to the cancellation line. The normal customer service operators might offer you a deal but it's the cancellation line that has all the power. Their main aim is not to lose you as a customer so that's where you're going to get the best offers to persuade you to stay. I've known people get savings of a whopping 80% by going through to the cancellation line.

Ask for freebies. Even if your contract isn't up for renewal yet, it's always worth ringing your provider and asking if there are any discounts, promotions or extras they can apply to your account. If you're finding your Wi-Fi is a little bit sluggish, then ring up and see if there's anything they can do about it. Their goal is to keep you as a happy customer for as many years as possible so often they will happily throw in a freebie.

Save on subscription services. Don't assume that you have to pay a set amount each month for subscription streaming services like Netflix and Now TV. There's always room for negotiation. As soon as you go to cancel, you might get an email offering you money off. I know that many of my Facebook group members have had some great discounts from Now TV. It's worth ringing them and saying, 'I'd like to stay with you but what can you offer me?'

HOW TO GET CHEAPER CAR INSURANCE

Pay annually. You can either pay your car insurance in monthly instalments or a lump sum. Paying monthly instalments might sound cost-effective and more manageable but in the long run, you end up paying a lot more. Monthly instalments are considered as loans by the insurer so you'll pay interest on them which can range between a whopping 25% and 36% Annual Percentage Rate (APR).

Choose the right job title. To calculate the cost of insuring you, insurance companies consider several factors and how you describe your job can make a huge difference. For example, as well as nurse there could be other nurse's jobs listed like community nurse, staff nurse or assistant nurse. Change the job title and see how the quotes differ. Never lie about your occupation or employment as that can invalidate your policy.

Add an experienced driver to your policy. It's illegal to say someone else is the main driver but it is legal to add a secondary driver. If you're considered a high-risk driver (you might have received lots of speeding tickets, been in an accident or you're aged 17–24), then adding an experienced driver with a clean driving licence to your policy can bring your premiums down. You'll need to get their permission before naming them.

Things that can lower your premiums. If you install a tracker, an immobiliser or an alarm to your car then it can help reduce your premiums.

Avoid auto-renewing. Don't let your insurer auto-renew your insurance cover. When you're approaching your renewal date, start haggling to get better deals, discounts or offers from rival insurance companies.

Cut the extras. Look at what's included in your car insurance quote and consider cutting the extras. For example, breakdown cover is normally offered as an extra, but you can probably get it cheaper elsewhere.

Holly's HACKS

Bill-reducing hacks

Make notes in your diary or phone calendar for when your contracts are up. Then you'll know it's time to ring your provider and negotiate a discount if they want to keep your custom.

Some banks offer 'rewards' if you opt for their premium bank account option . . .

I have a Halifax Ultimate Reward Account and get free travel insurance, free breakdown cover, mobile phone insurance and many more perks. Mine costs £15 a month but saves me so much as buying all the insurance separately would cost me triple that.

Unplug your devices when you're not using them. Some members of my money-saving Facebook group noticed that if they unplugged things like lamps and phone chargers, they were saving more money than when they were leaving them plugged in (even if the power was turned off).

EXPERT HACK!

This is one of my favourite hacks from blogger **Nicola** (**thefrugalcottage.com**), which she has let me share with you:

'Track everything. Incomings and outgoings. Knowing where your money is going and how much is coming in means you can change your spending habits and save more. Whether it's through a planner, app or a spreadsheet, find some way of tracking every penny in your budget. It will pay off.'

AMAZING MEMBERS' HACKS

'Go to savewatersavemoney.co.uk, put in your postcode and order free water-saving devices to go on your shower, toilet and taps to help save money on your water bill.'

'If you live on your own, you can get reductions on your council tax and water bills.'

'Most councils will let you spread your council tax over twelve months instead of ten, so the monthly cost is cheaper.'

'Have showers instead of baths. You'll save so much money and water.'

'I used Monopoly money to work out my budget. It was quite a wake-up call seeing what I had left after all my bills were paid.'

'Submit regular meter readings to make sure you're only paying for what you use. I was overpaying and got a lovely rebate of £350.'

'If you're elderly or on a low income, you can get a £140 discount off your electricity bill from the government's Warm Home Discount.'

'In the summer I use a solar phone charger. They're around £20 from Amazon.'

'If you're on benefits, you can get cold weather payments of £25 for every seven-day period of very cold weather between 1st November and 31st March.'

'Block draughts and invest in heavy curtains to keep the heat in during the winter. We decided to do this and saved £100 on our heating bill over the winter months.'

'Don't forget to have your boiler serviced. We didn't do this and ended up having to replace our boiler at a cost of £4,500. Paying for once-a-year maintenance would have saved our boiler and our money.'

'Bake a potato in half the time by putting a metal kebab skewer through the middle. It will save you electricity plus you don't have to wait as long for your dinner.'

'Use the power saving settings on any electronic devices you use (most people don't do this). It will extend the battery life on your devices and you'll get longer usage before having to plug-in.'

'I live in a flat and was using a tumble dryer to dry my clothes but decided to switch to a clothes airer. It saved me £300 on my electricity bill in a year and I found my clothes lasted longer.'

'To save on fuel, take heavy items out of your car. For example, if you have children and will be making a long journey without them, make sure you remove their car seats and any pushchairs in the boot. You'll use more petrol if your car is heavier.'

'Maintain your car tyres. Make sure you have the correct amount of air in your tyres as too little or too much air can increase your fuel consumption. It can also damage your tyres, meaning you'll have to replace them more often.'

'Check the seals on your fridge and freezer doors. I found mine were loose and leaking air, which meant they were using more electricity to keep my food chilled. Checking the seals could save you ££s on your electricity bills.'

'Ask your neighbours what Council Tax band they are in as so many people are on the wrong band. You might be entitled to a rebate if this is the case.'

Eating out on a budget (and my favourite baking hacks)

As a family of five, I know that eating out can be pricey but there are lots of ways to make it more affordable. We only tend to go to restaurants if there's a good offer on or we've got a deal or a voucher.

• •

HOW TO EAT OUT WITHOUT BREAKING THE BANK

Set up a dedicated email address to get newsletters from restaurants (you should already have done this if you followed my advice in the shopping chapters!), so they can send you promotional offers and vouchers. Normally they'll ask for your date of birth so they can send you a voucher for some sort of freebie on your birthday which is always nice.

Check if the restaurant you're going to has an app. Most of the large chains do and you can get offers and promotions on there. Or look for any regional apps that cover your area. For example, discount app Wriggle (getawriggleon.com) gives independent restaurants a chance to share last-minute offers with customers. It currently covers Bristol, Brighton, Cardiff, Bath and Birmingham.

Join restaurant loyalty schemes — one of my favourites is Nando's. Pick up a free card in store and each time you place an order over £7 you get a chilli point. Once you have enough chilli points, you can exchange them for free food.

If you eat out a lot, get a tastecard. It's a good investment as it gives you 50% off or two-for-one meals at over 6,000 restaurants. They offer trials, for example sixty days for £1, so you can try it out and after that you can choose to cancel it or pay the month or an annual membership.

Kids eat free. As a mum of three, this is one of my favourite offers and is a really good way to save money. Some eateries offer this all the time like the cafes in Asda and Morrisons. Others, such as Brewers Fayre and Beefeater, give kids a free breakfast or The Real Greek has kids eat free every Sunday. During school holidays, especially in the summer, most of the well-known chain restaurants will offer a 'kids eat free' promotion. It usually applies to a child who is twelve or under but check with each restaurant for details and see if there are any restrictions.

You might be able to order from your favourite restaurant 'to go' at a discount. Callum LOVES Frankie & Benny's and they have 40% off their menu when you click and collect it yourself via their app or website. Unless there's a really good offer on to encourage us to dine in then we'll normally get our favourite restaurant food to go as you save a lot.

Lunch is cheaper than dinner so think about the time that you're going out to eat. In most restaurants, the evening menu will start around 5.30pm. So, I make sure we get there at 5.15pm and put in our order to get the lunch/daytime price before the menu changes over to the more expensive evening menu. It's often cheaper to eat earlier than later and as long as your order goes to the kitchen before the new menu starts, you'll get the cheaper price.

The early bird catches the worm! Some restaurants that don't open until the evening do a cheaper early bird menu which works out good value and gives them another service of customers before they start to get busy later on. They normally run from around 5/5.30pm until 7pm but check with individual restaurants.

Check for pre-theatre menus. Callum and I always do this when we go to London. Many of the pubs and restaurants in the West End will do a set price, two or three-course pre-theatre menu in the early evenings. You don't have to be going to the theatre to take advantage of them and they're great value.

Don't spend money on expensive wine lists, go somewhere where you can BYOB (bring your own bottle). Some smaller restaurants that don't have an alcohol licence will let you bring your own drinks and charge you a small corkage fee per bottle, which works out much cheaper.

Check Groupon and Wowcher for deals. Local independent restaurants and sometimes chains will have promotions on there to encourage customers through the door. You can put in your postcode and search which local offers are available. We once got à la carte dining at Frankie and Benny's and got £35 worth of food each for £9.99 per person.

HOW NOT TO SPEND TOO MUCH IN A RESTAURANT

- ◎ Take cash if the place you're going to is not card only. Like shopping, when you take a credit or debit card it can be tempting to overspend. If your budget is £30, go to the cashpoint and withdraw the money and leave your cards at home. It will make you much more mindful of what you're ordering.

☺ Watch what you drink. Restaurants make their money on drinks, especially alcohol, so don't feel pressured into buying them. If you're on a strict budget, stick to water or look for deals that come with a drink included.

☺ Talking of water, make sure that you don't pay for it! If a restaurant serves alcohol, they're legally obliged to serve tap water free of charge so don't be afraid to ask. I always ask for a slice of lemon or lime to give mine a bit of flavour.

☺ Skip desserts and starters as they rack up your bill. I never buy starters — if you're on a budget, you don't really need them. Or if you really want them, then share them with your fellow diners.

☺ Take your time reading the menu. Restaurants will often put the most expensive items on the top right-hand corner of the menu because it's where your eyes fall first. So, make sure you look at the whole page — specials or set menus can often be on a different page. Don't be afraid to say if you need a little bit more time and ask if the prices are not on there.

☺ Set menus often work out better value. Choosing two or three set courses can often save you a lot more than ordering the same or similar items individually.

☺ If you haven't got a huge appetite or you're not mega hungry then order from the kids' menu. I do this all the time as I can't eat a lot because of my stomach condition. Most large chains don't seem to mind. Be mindful of how much things cost and what you get with them. Is it cheaper to buy one adult meal and split it between two kids or buy two kids' meals? Do they include any sides, desserts or drinks? Some restaurants also do two sizes of kids' meals, which is great as one of my girls hardly eats anything, so there's less waste with a smaller portion.

☺ Don't be afraid to ask for a 'to go' container if you can't eat all of your meal. Most restaurants do a takeaway service so they should have containers. Pop the leftovers in your fridge and you'll have a snack for the following day.

Holly's HACKS

Eating out hacks

If you're a **student,** you can get some great discounts — often up to 30% off your bill. Check if the restaurant you're going to offers a student discount and when it's available as often there are restrictions. The discount sometimes covers everyone who's dining (even if the people you're with are not students).

Don't waste leftover pizza that you take home from a restaurant. If you're reheating it in a microwave, then put a mug of water next to it as it stops it from going soggy.

EXPERT HACK!

Donna from www.**savvymumuk.co.uk** says, 'If you're eating out and you work for the NHS, ask if they do a NHS discount as many places do. Eat out during the week. Some restaurants have offers or cheaper menus during the week rather than at the weekend.'

AMAZING MEMBERS' HACKS

'Sign-up to Uber Eats and Deliveroo as they regularly send you money-off codes especially if you don't use the app for a while. Both me and my partner have accounts, so we get double the discounts.'

'I always google "(insert place you're eating at) discounts" to find current discounts.'

'Compare the Market offers two-for-one meerkat meals for a year when you buy travel insurance with them (which cost me £3 at the time). Loads of places accept it so it's well worth it.'

'The Gourmet Society card has saved me loads of money.'

Easy bakes from Extreme Couponing UK members

The best way to save money is to do it yourself. So instead of splashing out on an expensive dessert in a restaurant or buying sweet treats from cafes and supermarkets, why not make your own? I can always rely on my Facebook community to share some amazing recipes for easy, tasty bakes and these are the most popular. Each of these recipes has received over a million views and thousands of comments and 'likes'. They were so good they were even picked up by the national press. So why not give them a go yourself?

COCONUT FUDGE

Not only is this recipe super simple, the fudge will last a good while (that's if you can resist scoffing it all at once!).

You will need
300g icing sugar
300g desiccated coconut
1 x 405g tin of condensed milk
Food colouring (optional — I find red works best)
20cm square baking tin
Greaseproof baking paper

How to do it

1. Mix the icing sugar and desiccated coconut together. Make sure it's all blended together nicely.

2. Now add the condensed milk. Add it slowly and keep stirring the mixture.

3. Put half the mixture into a 20cm square baking tin lined with greaseproof paper. Mix a couple of drops of food colouring into the remaining mixture and then layer it over the top. This will make your fudge really POP when it's all cut up on a plate.

4. Put it in fridge for a few hours to set, checking after every 2 hours. The fudge should be slightly soft

to touch but firm enough not to have your finger sink straight through it.

5. Remove the tray from the fridge and carefully lift the paper and fudge out of the tin. Set the fudge aside on a chopping board and, with a large knife, carve it into pieces and store it in an airtight container. If you do have leftovers, it will keep in a cool place for up to 2 weeks.

 # MILKY BAR-STYLE PUDDING

This bad boy tray bake is so tasty. It can be made with lactose free substitutions too.

You will need
275g white chocolate spread
250g unsalted butter or spread alternative, melted
150g shortbread biscuits
300g icing sugar
300g Milky Bar chocolate (or any other brand of white chocolate that you like)
About 10 squares of milk chocolate
Topping of your choice (I like Milky Way Magic Stars)
20cm square baking tin
Greaseproof baking paper
A cocktail stick

How to do it
1. Whisk the white chocolate spread with the melted butter until it's completely blended.
2. Crush your shortbread biscuits. The best way to do this is by putting them into a sandwich bag and giving them a good bash with a rolling pin. In a bowl, add the crushed shortbread to the icing sugar and give them a quick stir.
3. Mix the buttery spread mix and the icing sugar and biscuits together until they make a paste. Scrape your mixture into a 20cm square baking tin lined with greaseproof paper. Spread evenly and put it into the fridge for 30 minutes to set.
4. Once the 30 minutes have passed, melt the white chocolate in a bowl. You can either microwave the chocolate or gently boil some water in a pan and rest the chocolate in a heatproof mixing bowl on top— don't let the bowl touch the water. Whichever method you use, make sure you don't overdo it as you don't want the chocolate to become tough and crystallise.
6. Pour and smooth the melted white chocolate over your chilled base. Then melt your squares of milk chocolate. When it's nice and runny, take your spoon and pour 'waves' across your dessert.
7. Take the cocktail stick and drag it just underneath the surface of

the melted chocolate. This will create a lovely marbled effect.

8. Now's the time to add any toppings if you choose. You can dot over chocolate buttons, Milky Way stars, sprinkles or add in wafers or just leave it plain.

9. Put your finished pudding back in the fridge for 1 hour.

10. Take your chilled dessert out of the fridge, cut it into bite-sized pieces and serve. This should last for 3 or 4 days stored in the fridge in an airtight container.

NUTELLA COOKIES

I honestly don't know many people who can resist these incredible home-made biscuits. They literally melt in your mouth. I like them best when they're fresh out of the oven along with a scoop of vanilla ice cream! De-licious!

Makes 12

You will need
12 heaped teaspoons Nutella
90g soft light brown sugar
115g unsalted butter (at room temperature)
1 large egg
210g self-raising flour
½ teaspoon baking powder
75g chocolate chips
2 baking trays (you need 1 for the nutella in the freezer and 1 for the cookies)
Greaseproof paper

How to do it

1. Scoop the Nutella on to a baking tray lined with greaseproof paper and slide them into the freezer until solid. This should take around 45 minutes, but it may take a little longer.

2. Preheat your oven to 190°C (170°C fan).

3. Take the sugar and butter and whisk them together until they're fluffy. Then crack in the egg and beat again until everything is smooth.

4. Now sift the flour and the baking powder into your mix. Sprinkle in your chocolate chips and mix until combined and doughy.

5. Scoop out 12 equal portions of the cookie dough (to keep everything roughly the same size use an ice-cream scoop) and place on a baking tray lined with greaseproof paper.

6. Flatten down each ball of dough with the back of a flour-dusted spoon until they are about 1cm thick. Add a frozen Nutella ball

into the centre of each cookie. Mould the sides of the cookie dough around the Nutella until it's completely covered and in a ball shape. Make sure you leave enough room in between each cookie as they'll expand in the oven. Bake for 11–13 minutes or until golden brown.

7. Set aside for at least 10 minutes for a warm cookie experience or 20 minutes for them to be properly cool. Eat and enjoy. Any leftovers should last for up to 3 days stored in an airtight container.

SLOW-COOKER CRUNCHIE FUDGE

This one is unbelievably easy and incredibly delicious. Maximum taste for minimum effort. What more could you want?

You will need
400g milk chocolate
1 x 397g can of condensed milk
15g unsalted butter
1 teaspoon vanilla essence
4 Crunchie bars (best kept refrigerated)
Greaseproof baking paper
30cm baking tin

How to do it
1. Put all the ingredients except for the Crunchie bars into a slow cooker.
2. Set the slow cooker to high and leave for 45 minutes with the lid off. Stir every 10–15 minutes to make sure everything is blending nicely until the 45 minutes are up.
3. Grab 3 of your Crunchie bars and chop them into small, bite-sized pieces. Make sure you cut each piece with one swift but careful motion to avoid the bar crumbling.
4. Add the Crunchie pieces to your slow-cooker mix. Pour the mix into a baking tin lined with greaseproof paper. Chop up the remaining Crunchie bar and sprinkle it over the top.
5. Pop the tray in the fridge to chill for about 6 hours to ensure it's set nicely.
6. Remove from the tray and cut into small chunks. Try not to eat the lot in one sitting. Any leftovers should last for up to 2 weeks stored in an airtight container.

Money-saving days out

Me, Callum and the kids love having a family day out, but if you don't plan ahead, they can work out to be really expensive. Here's what we do to save some cash.

• •

HOW TO SAVE MONEY ON ATTRACTIONS

Make a weekend of it — but don't stay on site

I absolutely love theme parks. As a teenager, me and some friends would go to Alton Towers a few times a year. Living in Great Yarmouth, we're at least three hours away from the nearest big attractions so if we do go somewhere like Alton Towers, LEGOLAND® or Chessington World of Adventures then we have to stay overnight. All the big theme parks have their own on-site hotels but they can be so expensive, especially at peak times like weekends and school holidays, when you're talking over £300 for one night. So, we look for a budget hotel like a Travelodge or a Premier Inn that offers a free kids' breakfast and is only a few minutes' drive to the park. We've gone to Alton Towers and got a £35 Travelodge room with a free breakfast for the girls which is a ten-minute drive from the park entrance.

Grown-ups go free

Look for the 'grown-ups go free' voucher for any Merlin attraction on packets of Kellogg's or Cadbury's products. For

For Summer

These cheap and easy hacks will save you money and help to keep your kids occupied during the long school holidays.

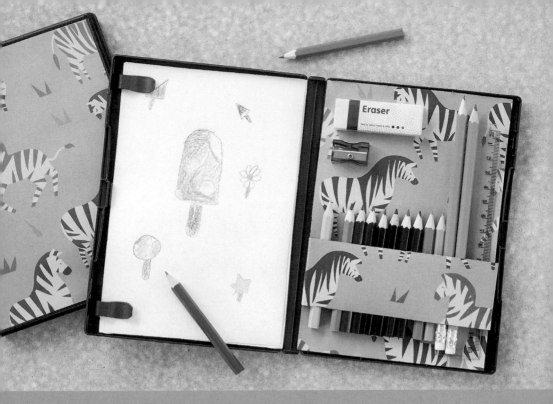

DIY DVD ACTIVITY CASE

If you're trying to think of ways to entertain the kids on a long journey, this clever little craft idea means that they'll always have something to do. The open DVD case will provide a hard surface for them to draw on as well as keeping their pens and pencils neat and tidy.

You will need
An old DVD or video game case
A piece of colourful card
PVA glue or glue dots
Basic stationery
Scraps of plain paper

How to do it
1. Start by removing the sleeve insert of the case. Most of these are plain on the reverse side so you can redecorate it with your own design.
2. Cut a piece of card to fit the inside of the case. Cut a strip of card that is 2cm longer than the backing card. Make 1cm folds on each end of the strip and stick the flaps to the back of the backing card. Your aim is to create a belt for pens and pencils. When the strip is stuck, glue the backing card to the inside of the case.
3. When the glue is dry, simply fill the case with stationery (felt-tip pens, colouring pencils and scrap paper) and pop it in your bag or the seat pocket of your car.

RAINBOW TOY SHELF

This was the first home craft I ever attempted. I managed to turn a plain, pine shoe rack into a rainbow storage area for my children's toys. Not only did it keep the room tidy, it looked really bright and cheerful too. I rotate the toys that I put on it every week to make sure that the kids play with everything.

You will need
Wooden flat-pack shoe rack
An assortment of tester
paint pots
Paintbrush

How to do it
1. Open the flat-pack shoe rack and separate the pieces.
2. Paint each piece of wood a colour of your choice and leave to dry.

Be careful to not use too much paint or the shoe rack will be tough to assemble later on.
3. Build your shoe rack according to the instructions.
4. Put a selection of toys on it and enjoy your new colourful storage.

DIY TWIG BIRDHOUSE

I love this summer craft as it not only gives the kids a good couple of hours to focus on a project but it also provides a brand-new home for a feathered friend.

You will need

2 sheets of cardboard (the thicker the better)
Ruler
PVA glue
Twigs/wooden lolly sticks
Scissors
Pen

How to do it

1. Grab a cardboard sheet and measure out a base size for your birdhouse. Cut out your shape (a square/rectangle works best), then cover it with a thin layer of PVA glue. (This will help protect it from the weather.)
2. Start sticking your twigs or lolly sticks around the edge of the cardboard base to build up the walls of your birdhouse. This process will take a LONG time as you need to give the glue a chance to set. Remember to leave space for the door/window to allow entry and exit points for the birds to get into their new home.
3. When the walls of the house are high enough (anything from 7.5–15cm is more than enough for a small birdhouse), cut a piece of card that will cover your house and then coat this in PVA glue too to weatherproof it.
4. When it is dry, glue sticks onto the top of your card roof to cover it.
5. When the roof is covered and the glue has set, coat the sticks once again with a thin layer of PVA glue to further help prevent leaks and offer more protection from the elements.
6. Stick the roof to the house with a little more glue.
7. Put your birdhouse in the garden and wait for the new residents to move in.

EASY CHANGE WALL ART

Have you ever put a picture up on your wall that you love but a few months later you've got a bit bored of it? If so, this is the project for you. It's insanely easy to make and it means that you can change your picture as often as you want depending on your mood, the season or current trends. Genius!

You will need
A picture frame of any size
A wallpaper sample
Scissors

How to do it

1. Take the back off your picture frame and remove whatever is currently in there.
2. Go to the decorating aisle of your local DIY store and take a strip of wallpaper off the sample roll.

These samples are normally free. You could also use a sheet of good-quality wrapping paper if you like the design but you'd need to stick it on some card or thicker paper to keep it flat.

3. Trim the paper so it fits in your frame and put it into place. Replace the back of the frame.
4. Hang your brand-new wall art and when you get bored, just get a new sheet of wallpaper.

MILK-BOTTLE ELEPHANTS

Unique, fun and a great rainy-day activity to occupy bored kids during the holidays. You can make whatever designs you want, and they always look so adorable.

You will need
An empty 1 litre milk bottle
Scissors
Scraps of paper, bits of foil or sweet wrappers
PVA glue
Card scraps Googly eyes

How to do it
1. Take your empty milk bottle and use a pair of scissors to cut it in half to remove the bottom.
2. Now cut small arches on all 4 sides on the bottle to create the 'legs' for the elephant.
3. Snip a small section of the base of the handle to create your elephant's trunk.
4. Start cutting the paper scraps, foil or sweet wrappers into strips, squares or any kind of shape you like to cover your elephant. When it comes to the lid, you can either cover it or decorate it to make a funky little hat.
5. Take the PVA glue and start sticking the scraps to the bottle until it's fully covered.
6. Cut 2 ears for the elephant from card scraps and decorate them with paper scraps and foil to match the body. Stick them on with a bit of glue.
7. When the elephant has dried, grab 2 googly eyes and stick them at the top of your elephant's trunk to create the face. They usually have a sticky pad on the back of them but if they don't you'll need to glue them in place.

DVD PLANT FEATURE

Upcycling is a great way to re-use a piece of furniture that's just been gathering dust. With a little bit of imagination, this old shelving unit has been transformed into a lovely new garden feature.

You will need
An old shelving unit or DVD rack
Sheets of old newspaper or an old towel or sheet
A pot of outdoor paint
Paintbrush
A few potted plants or garden ornaments of your choice

How to do it
1. Clear a small space in your garden and place your upcycled unit on a layer of newspaper or an old towel or sheet to catch any paint drips.
2. Paint the shelf in weatherproof exterior paint so it won't get ruined if you leave it outside.
3. Once it's dry, decorate it with anything from potted plants to garden gnomes.

every child's entry that that you pay for, one adult gets in for free. It's a great offer and significantly reduces the price of a day out for a family. It covers popular Merlin attractions including Alton Towers, Thorpe Park, LEGOLAND®, Chessington World of Adventures, Warwick Castle, Madame Tussauds, the London Eye and SEA LIFE centres. Using these vouchers and a budget hotel, it works out cheaper for us to travel to Alton Towers or LEGOLAND® and stay overnight than it does to go to our local theme park for the day.

Never pay at the gate

I can't bear it when people pay full price at the gate for an attraction because there's always a discount to be had. I live near a SEA LIFE centre and throughout the year there's always a Merlin offer or a 'buy one entry, get one free' discount running but you'd be surprised at how many people still pay full price. It's so easy to go to the Tourist Information office across the road or an Asda or Tesco store where they have a money-off voucher in a leaflet. One day I got so stressed about people paying full price, I got a wad of vouchers and handed them out in the queue!

If there's an odd number of you . . .

If you're a family of five like mine, it can feel like you're missing out as the 'buy one entry, get one free' deal doesn't work if you've got an odd number of children. But all you have to do is ask in the queue if there's anyone who doesn't have a voucher who'd like to go in with you and then you can split the cost. When I went to Alton Towers with my mates, we didn't always have even numbers, so we'd always find someone in the queue who was on their own or another group with odd numbers and pair up, so everyone was covered by a voucher.

Cash out your Clubcard

Some loyalty cards, like the Tesco one, allow you to redeem your points to get discounts on days out. Use the Clubcard website to search the attractions where you can use them.

Book online to save

If you're heading to a smaller theme park or attraction that's local to you and doesn't have any regular offers, check their website for discounts. You'll normally save money by booking online and they'll often have an early bird discount or a group discount which can work out good value if two families are going together.

Check your kid's school bag

If your child brings home a magazine from school, such as *Primary Times*, check inside for special offers on attractions. Also look out for competitions where you can win free entry too as these sorts of competitions don't get a huge amount of entries so you stand a good chance of winning.

Look for leaflets

If you're on holiday or even in your local area, check attraction leaflets for discount codes or coupons. You often find these in hotels, supermarkets, service stations and Tourist Information offices. If you're at a Tourist Information office, it's always worth asking them if they have any vouchers for the attraction you're hoping to visit as sometimes they'll keep coupons with the biggest discounts behind the counter because they're limited.

Reach out on social media

If you're thinking about visiting an attraction, then contact them on social media. Tell them that you're planning a day out and politely ask if they have any deals or discounts available. Nine times out of ten they'll offer you something because they know that once they get you through the door, you'll spend more money. I did a survey with my Facebook group members and worked out that if a family of four go to a theme park for the day, the least they're likely to spend in the park is £60.

Travel by train

Most railway companies will offer you a discount when you travel to an attraction by train. Check out the page on your train operator's website to find out which attractions you can get discounts on. You have to print out a voucher and show a valid rail ticket when you get to the entrance.

Get an annual pass

If you're going to visit a theme park or an attraction more than a couple of times a year, it's probably worth buying an annual pass. Merlin do an annual pass that will get you a year's entry into thirty of their attractions plus discounts on food, retail and on-site accommodation. They can cost from £139 per person and there are occasionally discounts on them. But what a lot of people don't realise is that you can get an annual pass for just one of their attractions. For example, I once bought an annual pass to Alton Towers for the same price as a single day's entry. If you're going to go more than once, it's good value for money. Check each attraction's website for details of their annual passes. The best time to buy annual passes is off-season (November to March) as there will be often discounts available.

HOW TO SAVE WHEN YOU VISIT AN ATTRACTION

Don't buy food in the park

The food at attractions is always eye-wateringly expensive and not that great in my opinion. If you can, avoid going into the restaurants because the kids always want the overpriced novelty items (giraffe waffles or Lego-shaped pies anyone?!). So, take a packed lunch with you and eat it at the park. The only downside to this is that you have to carry your cool bag and food around with you all day. We leave it in the car if the car park's not too far away and and have a picnic there at lunchtime.

Another option is to have a look at the local area before you go on a day out and see if there's a supermarket or a pub close to the park entrance. This doesn't work if you're somewhere remote like Alton Towers and there's nothing around it. But outside my local theme park in Lowestoft there's a Harvester and a Tesco. So, we either drive out of the park and get a meal deal at Tesco or go to the Harvester where the kids eat for free. We did this with a Beefeater outside of Chessington too. We had a lovely big lunch and it was so much more affordable than eating in the park.

Avoid the gift shop

If you step one foot in the gift shop, then before you know it your kids will be begging you for a cuddly toy or rubber snake that will end up discarded in a few weeks' time. If they're desperate to buy something, then get a keyring or a magnet that you can put on the fridge as a souvenir instead.

Pin badges are a good buy as they can increase in value over the years if you keep hold of them.

Pack snacks

With kids, you can never have too many snacks and make sure you hide them in your bag otherwise they'll have finished them by 10am. Snacks at attractions are expensive and you know your child is going to walk past a sweet stall or an ice-cream cart and suddenly decide that they're hungry. Bring some multipacks of crisps or some iced gems (you can get six packets for £1 in Poundland).

Don't buy drinks in the park

Take a reusable water bottle that you can fill up at the water fountains around the park (although they can be heavy to lug around all day) or ask for a free cup of iced water at the kiosks and restaurants.

FREE OR CHEAP DAYS OUT

☺ Check websites, such as dayoutwiththekids.co.uk, to find free museums, attractions and events in your area.

☺ Search for regional events, such as fetes and festivals. You'll often get leaflets in local shops or supermarkets that will list all the free events throughout the year in your area or do a quick Google search. These events are great for kids and often involve free performances and arts and crafts.

☺ Split the cost of a day out with some friends and do something different. Instead of going to a theme park, we hired a boat with our mates. It was £150 for the whole day and you could have up to twenty people on board, so it worked out quite inexpensive. We brought a picnic and spent the day sailing around.

☺ Get cheap cinema tickets. Most cinemas show films on a Saturday morning, sometimes for as little as £1 a ticket. They normally brand it for kids, but anyone can go — I know loads of adults who love Disney or Pixar movies. Remember to bring your own drinks and snacks.

☺ If the zoo or safari park is too pricey, then take the kids to a city farm. They're free to get into although donations are welcome. Well known ones include Bath City Farm, Stonebridge City Farm in Nottingham and Surrey Docks and Vauxhall City farms in London.

FREE ACTIVITIES FOR ADULTS

Comedy and open mic nights

Google free comedy nights in your area as you'll often find evenings where new comedians test out their jokes. Or you can see well-known comedians doing warm-up gigs where they practise their material ahead of a big tour for a fraction of the cost. Open mic nights in pubs are also a nice way to get free entertainment.

Volunteering at festivals

Look at volunteering at shows or big festivals so you get your ticket paid for. To be a volunteer at Glastonbury, you have to go through a group or charity and complete a certain number of hours — normally three lots of eight-hour shifts — to get your ticket paid for. There are also social media events throughout the year where you can meet your favourite YouTube stars and they rely on volunteers to help backstage.

Wine tastings and beer festivals

There are so many beer and wine festivals and food markets that will let you try samples for free. Some people might be embarrassed but they're open events so anyone can go, and you don't have to feel pressured to buy anything.

Free bingo, horse racing or casino nights

Bingo halls, casinos and racecourses will often have offers on where you can get a free three-course meal and a bet on a race, a game of bingo or roulette. All of these offers are designed to get you through the door in the hope that once you've had your free food, drinks and bet, then you'll stay on and gamble more. If you have a weakness for gambling and/ or are on a budget, these sorts of offers are not for you! But if you think you can refrain from gambling after your complimentary bet then they're a good way of enjoying a free night out.

Discount theatre tickets

Apart from Taylor Swift, the only music that I listen to are songs from musicals. I'm obsessed! So, any time I go to London I always look to see if there's a matinee or an evening performance that I can go to. But West End shows can be incredibly expensive — you're talking about £70 or more a ticket for some of them. So, I always go on websites, such as

TodayTix and lastminute.com, to find cheap, on-the-day tickets. I particularly like lastminute.com because they do meal and show deals that are great value. We went to see my favourite musical *Legally Blonde* five times towards the end of its West End run and we got tickets AND a meal before the show for £20 per person.

You can also enter theatre lotteries — these can be on the day at the theatre or a week before online. We entered the online lottery for Disney's Aladdin and won front row tickets for £25. You can also go to the TKTS booth in Leicester Square for last-minute discounted theatre tickets. Many theatres, such as the Young Vic, The Barbican and The National, also offer discounted tickets (sometimes for £5 or £10) if you're under twenty-six.

Holly's HACKS

Day-out savings hacks

Buy some concentrated squash like Robinsons SQUASH'D to take with you on a day out. You get twenty servings of squash in one tiny bottle. I always have one of these in my bag if we're out at an attraction to squirt into a free iced water and it tastes amazing. It's so strong you only need a tiny squirt and it will save you a fortune. Aldi does its own version too.

Holly's HACKS

If you're disabled or have a hidden disability or condition, then theatres will often offer you a discount on your tickets. Phone individual theatres to ask for details. Normally you have to show proof of your disability (I have an autism card from my local council), and you will often get two tickets for the price of one so your carer can go free. I've found most local and London theatres will offer a disability discount as well as being accommodating, like finding me a seat at the end of an aisle so I can get out quickly without disturbing people.

EXPERT HACK!

Here's a great one from **Jonathan Gutteridge (themoneyshed. co.uk)**: 'Don't pay to go to the cinema. There are loads of ways to see films for free or get a discount on your tickets. Take a look at Sweet Sundays, Free Movies UK (FMUK), Sun Savers and Showfilmfirst. There is also Meerkat Movies — a rewards scheme for customers of comparethemarket.com that offers two-for-one cinema tickets.'

AMAZING MEMBERS' HACKS

'Take a look at kidspass.co.uk for all sorts of discounts for days out.'

'It's worth investing in a National Trust membership for family days out. We use ours all the time and loads of places have free events on in the holidays.'

'I look on eBay for cheap tickets for days out. People will often sell tickets on there if they've booked advanced tickets but can no longer go to the attraction or show.'

'Check out daysout.co.uk for discounts on days out and two-for-one offers.'

Making budget-busting occasions more affordable . . .

. . . Holidays and travel

Here are my top ten tips to help you save money on your holidays.

1. Don't hire a satnav

When we went to Orlando and picked up our hire car it was $19 (around £15) a day to hire a satnav, which can really add up over a two-week holiday. But you don't need to do that as there are loads of free apps that will turn your smartphone into a satnav. My favourite is Navmii which covers 200 countries — you just download the version for the country that you're visiting. If you don't want to pay for data roaming on your smartphone while you're away, then use Google Maps instead. You can use it offline as long as you've downloaded the maps that you need in advance.

2. Find cheap fuel

If you're driving around an area that you don't know and you need to get fuel, there are free apps that tell you where you can get the cheapest fuel. In the UK there's an app called PetrolPrices and the US version is GasBuddy. You type in your postcode or allow it access to your location and the app lists every petrol station in the area where you are and tells you the cheapest place to buy petrol or diesel. It's really useful when you have to drop a hire car back at the end of your trip and you need to find somewhere to fill the tank up. Petrol near airports can be really expensive so these apps can save you quite a lot of money. I highly recommend using them all the time, even when you're not on holiday.

3. Don't rent a pushchair

If you're going on holiday where there's a theme park, don't rent a buggy. There's a lot of walking involved in theme parks so parents will often hire a stroller for slightly older children who wouldn't normally have one any more at home. However, it can be expensive — at Disney World, Florida it was $15 per day to rent a single stroller or $31 for a double when we went. Instead, go to a Walmart, five minutes' drive from Disney and buy a lightweight foldable pushchair/buggy/stroller for $28. As well as saving you a fortune, at the end of your holiday you can give it to another family to use so it's a nice random act of kindness too.

4. Try glamping

If you don't want to rough it in a tent but you don't want to pay the high prices of a caravan, then try glamping. I'm not a camping fan but even I can be persuaded by glamping. You can get some really luxurious tents that come with proper beds, fridges and even bathtubs. Check Wowcher and Groupon for some great deals.

5. Get discounted rail travel

Some people think that you can only get a Railcard if you're a student or a pensioner but there are actually nine different Railcards available — including Two Together, Family and Friends and a 26–30 Railcard. If you're going to travel by train at least a couple of times within a year, then it's worth getting a railcard as you will make your money back as well as getting discounted rail tickets.

6. Upgrade your train ticket

Use the Seatfrog app to bid on empty first-class seats. From twenty-four hours before you travel, use the app to search for your train journey and it will tell you what upgrades are available. You start bidding in an auction or you can buy an upgrade outright. You can sometimes upgrade your standard class ticket to first for as little as £5. The app covers tickets on Great Western, Avanti West Coast, CrossCountry and London North Eastern railways.

7. Get your own taxi

Never get the taxis that wait outside train stations or airports as they're usually the most expensive. They pay extra to get a special licence to be able to wait at the ranks and you will always pay a premium for their services. It's worth walking for a few minutes to flag down another taxi which usually works out much cheaper. Try Uber too.

8. Use comparison sites to find hotels

If I'm looking for a hotel, then I always use comparison websites hotels.com and ebookers.com as they offer great reward schemes. When you book through hotels.com you collect one stamp for every night that you stay. When you collect ten stamps you get one free reward night. If you book through ebookers.com you can get 10% cashback on your bookings. You can also use a cashback site at the same time for extra savings.

9. Book a flexible rate

If you're booking a budget hotel like a Travelodge or a Premier Inn, don't book a room on the saver rate (unless you're 100% certain you'll be using it). If it gets closer to the time and you have to cancel your stay, you're going to lose your money. Book the flexible rate, then a few days before you go, check if you can still get the saver rate. If it's still available, then book that and cancel the flexible rate which you can do up to 1pm on the day you arrive. Normally the flexible rate is around £15 more.

10. Try a Top Secret® hotel

This is a great section of lastminute.com that often offers rooms at four- or five-star hotels for up to 40% less. The only catch is, you don't know the name of the hotel until after you book it. You can find secret hotel deals across the UK and also internationally including Europe and the US. Callum and I have done this a couple of times and we've got a really posh hotel in central London worth £300 plus for £99 bed and breakfast. It's a really good money saver. There are also sneaky ways to find out which hotel it might be before you book. Copy and paste bits of the hotel description into Google and along with the area, and with a bit of detective work you're likely to be able to work out which hotel it is.

HOW TO SAVE ON FLIGHTS

- ☺ It generally works out cheaper to fly out on a Tuesday or Wednesday.
- ☺ Always clear the cookies on your browser if you're looking at the cost of certain flights, otherwise the price may increase.
- ☺ Use a comparison website like Skyscanner to compare the cost of different airlines. Using a combination of airlines sometimes works out cheaper than just using the same one for your journey there and back.

- ☺ Track your flights for a couple of weeks or more before you buy them to see if you notice any patterns. The prices of flights can go up and down and there are often certain days and times when the prices drop slightly.
- ☺ Always book your hold luggage in advance and not at the airport otherwise you'll pay a premium.
- ☺ If you buy anything from Duty Free, then you can use that bag as additional hand luggage.
- ☺ If you're flying with a budget airline, buy food before you get on board. The prices on board are insanely expensive and often the food isn't great quality. Go to an M&S or Boots in the airport terminal and get a meal deal for £3.50 to take on the flight.

How I took eight people to a Haven Holiday Park for £7

This is one of my favourite hacks of all time. I managed to use a holiday park's facilities for a FRACTION of the cost. If you want to stay in a holiday park like Haven for a week in the summer, it could cost you around £800 or more for a caravan. However, what a lot of people don't know is that some of these sites have a camping section where you can pay for a pitch. It makes it a much cheaper holiday — you book a pitch and bring your tent and you can still use the same facilities as the people in the caravans but it's a tiny fraction of the cost.

I have a Haven holiday park near me, and I discovered that I could get a pitch for £7 a night for up to eight people. But what I then realised is that even if I bought a pitch for a night, I didn't have to use it and instead we could get a really cheap day out. So, I booked a pitch for one night, eight of us checked in and it meant we could use all the park facilities. There was an indoor and outdoor pool, a big play area and we had passes so we could enjoy all the entertainment. We had such a fun day out and the kids loved it and we paid less than a pound each for it. It was cheaper than eight of us paying to go to our local swimming pool and we got a whole day and evening's entertainment. It's a cheap holiday but an even cheaper day out.

EXPERT HACKS!

My mates **Leigh** and **Nick** from **The Lodge Guys** channel on YouTube have shared these hacks with us:

If you're planning to book with the website Holiday Extras, to get a discount ensure you have signed up to their site, browse for your booking whether it's airport car parking or an airport hotel, get an initial quote then close the app. Within twenty-four hours you should receive an email from them offering you a discount on your searched booking, usually in the region of 10–15%.

When you're hiring a car, especially in Spain, you'll find the best deals are with local independents in the resort where you're staying rather than big car hire chains. For example, Cabrera Medina (cabreramedina.com) in the Canaries offer a rate nearly 50% cheaper than the bigger companies. Most local car hire companies have booths in the terminal building at the airport.

If you're visiting a country and you don't speak the language, use Google translate which has a built-in, real-time translator. You can even look at a sign through the app and it will translate it for you.

When you're packing for your holiday, roll your clothes and use packing cubes. Doing this will give you 30–40% more space in your suitcase plus your clothes won't be creased.

To avoid buying or bringing lots of adapters when you travel, take a UK four-plug extension cable and one travel adapter. You're not allowed to do this on cruises but it's great if you're in a hotel or apartment.

Don't book trips and excursions through your holiday company if you're on a package deal as you'll pay a premium. Use an app like Viator.com to book directly with local guides. You'll often get a better price and a more personal service, as you pay the guides directly, so they're motivated to give you a better experience. Often the groups are smaller too.

And from travel vloggers **Luke** and **Rich (L & R Dreaming)**, we have this hack:

Download the app RED by Dufry — it's a free app that will get you immediate discounts in Duty Free shops.

Stephie and **Dave** from **Krispy Smore** on YouTube suggest:

Always have an empty water bottle with you before you go through airport security as all airports have free water filling stations.

Have a look at beauty magazines in the airport as some will have make-up and skincare samples inside that could last for the length of your holiday. It will give you something to read on the plane too.

AMAZING MEMBERS' HACKS

'Splitting train tickets can make a train journey much cheaper than going direct. I use traintickets.com as it's a simple way to find split tickets.'

'Download the app for the airport that you're travelling from as they have special offers for shops and restaurants.'

'I've saved a small fortune using secretflying.com. It shows you all the dates you can get super cheap flights. Last year I managed to get £20 flights to Alicante.'

'I swapped travelling by train for going by bus or coach. The modern coaches come with air conditioning and Wi-Fi and even though it takes slightly longer to reach your destination, the savings are worth it. I saved over £500 last year.'

'Every year *The Sun* newspaper has tokens you can collect to get a £9.50 holiday.'

... Your wedding

When Callum and I got engaged in 2011, it was him not me who had the dream of a big white church wedding. Mollie was only six months old and because of my autism and social anxiety, I would have been happy to nip down to the local registry office with a few close family and friends. In the end, I couldn't deny the poor man his special day.

But weddings are pricey and as soon as we started planning it, my money-saving instincts well and truly kicked in. I managed to win £10,000 worth of prizes including wine for our reception and a cruise for our honeymoon and I haggled the cost of our reception down too. It meant a £10,000 wedding cost us £3,500 all in. This section could be a whole book in itself but here are my top ten ways to help you save on your big day.

MY TOP TEN WEDDING TIPS THAT WILL SAVE YOU MONEY

1. Go virtual with your invites

Wedding invitations can cost hundreds if you get them professionally designed and printed. To save money, email or text your 'save the date' and use a digital invite. You can hire someone to design and personalise a wedding e-invite for you, which you can then attach to an email to send to all of your guests. Check websites, such as etsy.com or fivver.com, where you can get a digital invite made from as little as £4. Or to save even more money, design one yourself. Use a free graphic design platform, such as canva.com. It's easy to navigate and there are lots of set templates and design ideas and it won't cost you a penny.

2. Enter competitions

There are so many competitions in bridal magazines and they're well worth entering, especially the ones in regional magazines where the prizes are all offered by local suppliers. Because they're only open to people getting married within a certain timescale, you've got a good chance of winning them. I won ten competitions in the run up to our wedding through wedding magazines.

3. Make your own favours

Giving each of your guests a favour at their table setting can be very costly, particularly if you're having a big wedding. A really economical way to make your own favours is to buy some cheap chocolate bars, take the outer wrapper off leaving just the foil, then use free software like canva.com to design your own label. You can personalise it with your names and wedding date. Then in one of the chocolate bars at each table put a free drinks voucher for that person to use at the bar. It's a gentle way of letting guests know that there isn't a free bar later, plus it encourages people to chat and mingle if they don't already know each other.

For our wedding, I personalised the label on packets of Love Hearts with a template I found online. A hundred Love Hearts cost me £6 on eBay so it was really cheap to do, and it looked great.

4. Sweet treats

People like to have a bit of a novelty item at their wedding reception for after dinner. Instead of forking out to hire an ice-cream van or a candyfloss machine, I made my own sweet buffet. I bought big tubs of pick and mix sweets at a wholesaler for around £4 a tub. Then I went on eBay and got scoops, striped paper bags and some glass vases and bowls. It looked amazing when it was all laid out and my guests absolutely loved it. The best thing was it only cost me around £20.

5. Get baking

I wanted to have a wedding cake, but I got a quote for £800 for a three-tier one. Then I found out M&S sold wedding cakes, but to buy enough tiers to serve a hundred people, it would still have been around £200. In the end I got a cake stand, ordered the top tier fruitcake for £8 from M&S and then asked family and friends to bake cupcakes to fill up the rest of the tiers — I am lucky as I know a few brilliant bakers who enjoyed pitching in. We cut the top tier for the photos and the different coloured cupcakes underneath it looked really beautiful. It was convenient too as our guests could just come up and grab a cupcake rather than us having to slice a whole cake up.

6. Find a floristry student

Wedding flowers can cost hundreds of pounds so why not approach your local college to see if any of the floristry students are willing to do them for you? They will have been making arrangements as part of their course and it's a great opportunity for them as they'll be able to feature it in their portfolio. My mum did my flowers, but friends have used students and got all their bouquets, buttonholes and table arrangements for £150—200.

7. Get a honeymoon as a gift

We had a gift table at our wedding, and we got so many lovely pressies, but we also ended up with three toasters. Now there are so many things you can do to avoid that. Set up an Amazon wishlist with gifts in a range of prices so guests can get something that you genuinely want and will use.

Some travel agents also offer schemes where guests can contribute to the cost of your honeymoon. A lot of people don't have any money left to spend on their honeymoon after they've paid for the wedding, so this is a great idea.

8. Tie the knot 'off peak'

You'll pay a premium for your venue if you get married on a weekend, so get married on a weekday instead and save thousands. Or choose an off-peak time of year for your big day. I got married in October and there was a lot more availability than in spring or summer and it was cheaper too. You've got a little bit more wiggle room to haggle as places aren't so booked up.

9. Don't mention the 'w' word

When you're getting quotes from people, such as DJs, try to avoid saying it's for a wedding if you can. You'll find as soon as you mention that you're getting married, you'll be quoted a higher price. If you're booking a DJ and a friend has recommended them it's always worth asking if they do a 'refer a friend' discount.

10. Book a one-way car

I wasn't bothered about having a fancy wedding car to take me to the church so I bought a ribbon for my mum's Skoda so she could give me a lift. But a few days before the wedding, I phoned a few car-hire places just to see if I could get a last-minute deal and I got a beautiful classic wedding car for £50 instead of £300.

If I hadn't have got that for a bargain price, then I probably wouldn't have bothered. No one would see me arrive as everyone was in the church already. Car-hire places often charge per hour and if they take you to the church, they'll charge you for the time they spend waiting outside during the service. So instead, get a friend or family member to take you to the church then hire a wedding car to pick you up and take you to the reception. That way, you won't pay for any waiting time and you'll only have one journey, plus you'll have a nice car for the photos.

HOW TO SAVE CASH ON YOUR WEDDING DRESS

Try a charity shop. Oxfam have a specialist online wedding dress store where you can get up to 80% off. Charities, such as The Red Cross, Barnardo's and Oxfam, also have selected shops that have bridal sections.

Look at the sale rail in bridal shops. Most bridal shops will have a rail of discontinued designs or ex-display dresses that you can buy for a heavily discounted price and get dry-cleaned if necessary.

Buy second hand. I went to a bridal shop and found a dress I loved but it had to be ordered nine months in advance and I didn't have enough time. I went home and found the exact same dress for sale on eBay and got it for £400 compared to £1,200 in the shop. If you love a particular dress or a designer, then it's always worth checking to see if you can buy it second hand.

Hire a dress. Why buy for one day when you can hire? It's a way to get a designer dress at a much cheaper price. vonleebridalhire.com have dresses to hire from £195, which also includes a tiara, veil and underskirt.

Wedding hacks

Instead of having a three-course meal at your wedding reception, **serve afternoon tea**. It's a way to make buffet sandwiches look more elegant and sophisticated plus it will save you thousands.

Don't pay a fortune for private dance lessons for your first dance. You can go on YouTube and find professional dancers who have choreographed whole dances for wedding songs. Often, they will post videos, teaching you the dance step-by-step. You can watch them with your partner and learn your dance at home rather than paying hundreds of pounds for private lessons.

Ask your venue if you can **bring your own wine** for the reception and just pay corkage. You can then buy the wine wholesale.

AMAZING MEMBERS' HACKS

'Buy a money pot (a money box that you can only open by smashing it) and start selling anything you don't want or need any more and put the money straight into the pot. My hubby and I did this, and we ended up with almost £1,000 by our wedding day.'

'Don't get hung up on little things like chair covers. It's an added expense that no one else even really notices on the day.'

'Never take the first price offered and even haggle on your wedding dress. My dress was originally £1,350, but it was going to the sale rack for £800 and I haggled and bought it for £595 including alterations.'

'Get friends and family to help out with the wedding instead of buying you gifts. One friend made a four-tier cake, another iced it. My parents' friends made all the food for the buffet, a friend hired the room and my then future mother-in-law made the bridesmaid dresses. It felt like everyone had played a part in our day and it made it really special.'

'Use Pinterest to get ideas to make your invitations, place settings and table decorations.'

... Have an amazing Christmas

Christmas is probably *the* most expensive time of the year. It can also be a stressful time for many people and the pressure to go all out and have the perfect Christmas can push them into debt. In fact, a recent survey found that the average British consumer spends just under a whopping £1,000 during the festive period. My budget is always £300, and I never go over that. To find out how I do it, follow my guide and you and your family can have a lovely Christmas without spending thousands of pounds.

HOW TO SAVE MONEY ON YOUR CHRISTMAS FOOD SHOP

Set a budget

Work out your overall budget and what you can realistically afford to spend on your Christmas food shop. My budget is normally £100. This should also include snacks and alcohol. It's Christmas, so you're going to want to buy extra luxury items that you wouldn't normally have. Our tradition is we always have a Terry's Chocolate Orange and After Eights after our Christmas dinner. Make sure you include all of those festive treats in your budget.

Meal plan

Meal plans often go out of the window over the festive season, but you should still plan out the two weeks covering Christmas and New Year. Work out which meals you'll be eating at home, how many people you've got to cater for and the ingredients you'll need. Now's the time to google some recipes so you can make use of all your leftovers. Make sure everything is on your shopping list — even the basics like potatoes, sprouts and carrots can easily be forgotten in a crowded supermarket.

Shop with cash

Paying by cash wherever possible and not taking cards is always a good idea if you're shopping on a strict budget but especially at Christmas when there's more chance of overspending. The supermarkets are playing Christmas music, you're feeling festive and the temptation is to fill up your trolley. Use the handheld scanners to monitor what you're spending as you go round the store or the use the calculator on your phone. It's also a good idea to choose a smaller trolley. If you get a bigger one, you're more likely to fill it. With the smaller, more shallow trollies it's easier to see what you've put in there.

Avoid novelty items

There are so many novelty products in the shops at Christmas designed to tempt you. Before you know it, you'll have put those limited-edition, turkey-flavoured crisps or the mince-pie gin into your trolley. You pay so much more for these festive one-offs and seasonal packaging so if you're on a strict budget, then they're best avoided.

If you do have money in your budget for novelty items, then you'll probably pick them up cheaper in the bargain stores. Last year Home Bargains had gin and tonic crisps for 99p and Parma Violet gin for £8 a bottle instead of £20 in the supermarkets.

Try luxury ranges from budget supermarkets

Every year, newspapers and magazines do taste tests where they rate the festive food products from all the stores and supermarkets. Often the luxury ranges from Aldi and Lidl come out on top – last year Aldi's mince pies were rated higher than many of the leading supermarkets. The budget supermarket ranges might not look as luxurious but the actual product tastes great and they're so much cheaper. You could save up to £3 on a box of mince pies alone.

Buy in advance

Around Christmastime some supermarkets hike up the price of popular products. So, if you know you're going to need certain things like gravy granules, cranberry sauce and stuffing mix for your festive lunch, buy them a few months before Christmas to avoid any seasonal increase. It might only be 10 or 20p but it can all add up.

Buy booze from the bargain stores

A lot of people don't realise that B&M and Home Bargains both have alcohol sections and you can get some great bargains if you're stocking up for Christmas. Home Bargains sometimes have brand-name wines for half the price you'd pay in the supermarket.

Use your leftovers

If you have any leftover food from Christmas, make sure that you use it all up. There are all sorts of imaginative meals you can make with turkey rather than just putting it in sandwiches or alternatively, freeze it and use it later. Make a turkey curry, put leftover veg into omelettes and quiches or freeze them to put in pies and casseroles.

WHEN AND WHERE TO BUY CHRISTMAS TOYS

I have one golden rule when it comes to buying toys for Christmas presents. I buy them throughout the year for everyone apart from my own children. If I see a good bargain, I'll buy it and put it in my stockpile. So, when it comes to Christmas, I'll have built up a good selection of toys to give to family and friends that I've already paid for. Every year I spend up to £100 on each of my girls (Cloud's too young at the moment) so I can buy them the toys on their letters to Santa. The only way I can do that is by buying everyone else's presents throughout the year and spreading the cost. The Christmas craze toys that my girls might want are not likely to be discounted.

If you shop smartly throughout the year then you can give someone a toy that's worth £20 that you've bought for a fiver. If it's a particularly good bargain, I'll buy two for my stockpile — one for Christmas and one for a birthday present.

Where to find the best toy bargains

Amazon. Use the discount finders like jungle-search.com (as mentioned on page 40) to find the discounted toy deals. If you check that every few days, you can pick up some great bargains throughout the year.

Bargain stores. Stores like The Range, Home Bargains and B&M are great places to pick up bargain toys. You can get brand name toys, such as LEGO®, Playmobil and Play-Doh, sometimes with up to 80% off. These tend to be overstock or discontinued toys that the manufacturers want to be sold off. They're generally one-off bargains so if you see something, grab it and put it in your stockpile for Christmas.

One word of warning — sometimes the recommended retail price (RRP) can be slightly inflated so you think you're getting a much bigger discount than you actually are. If you're not sure that you're getting a genuine bargain, google the item while you're in the store to see how much it was being sold for at full price.

Retailer eBay outlets. Another way to save money on toys is to look at the outlet stores that many of the large shops have on eBay. Argos have an eBay outlet where they sell off items, including toys, that have been discontinued and are not going to be in their catalogues any longer. Other stores that sell toys and have eBay outlets are Tesco, Debenhams and Sports Direct (good for outdoor toys). Go to ebaystores. co.uk.

Buy second hand. Look on local Facebook selling pages for bargains. After Christmas, people will be selling unwanted presents that are often unopened and still in their packaging. These Facebook groups are also a good place to find second-hand toys for babies. Babies and toddlers don't know if the toys that you give them at Christmas are new or not — they're probably more interested in the wrapping paper or the box. Normally they're in a great condition because babies grow out of them so quickly — just disinfect them before you give them to your baby. One of my biggest bargains on a Facebook selling page was a bouncy castle that was £150 new, and I got it for £30. We've been using it for five years and my girls have had so much fun out of it.

MY TOP TEN FESTIVE TIPS THAT WILL SAVE YOU MONEY

1. Buy a reusable advent calendar

Instead of a chocolate advent calendar, buy a wooden one that you can reuse. Every year the bargain stores sell them for around £5 and they're either a train with numbered carriages or a wooden house. They're good quality and they'll last year after year which is why they always sell out. It's great for children with allergies or intolerances as you can fill the drawers with anything you want from sweet treats and craft supplies to little toys or stationery. You can even do them for adults with different varieties of teabags, make-up, toiletries, seeds or even miniature bottles of alcohol.

2. Enter advent competitions

Most of the big retailers have advent competitions. These are 24-hour flash competitions that work a bit like an advent calendar. You open an email or go on to their website to reveal that day's prize. They're worth entering as you've got more chance of winning as they're only on for a limited time. I've won toys and games over the years which have been great to give as Christmas presents. If you've got a spare ten minutes a day to enter a few it's really worth it.

3. Only buy for the kids

Money is a tricky thing to talk about but if you're worried about spending too much at Christmas then talk to your friends and family and you'll probably find they're in the same position. People do struggle and if you've got a big family it can be expensive to buy a present for everyone. Talk to family and suggest that maybe this year you just buy

For Autumn

Autumn is one of my favourite seasons. It's a time to get cosy and curl up inside and of course Callum, the kids and I love the excitement of Halloween. These crafts will help transform your home and keep your little ones busy too.

LEAF LIGHTS

This is a way to create some classy, gentle mood lighting and make your house look really cosy and autumnal.

You will need
An empty glass jar
Autumn leaves (yellow, red or orange leaves would be ideal)
PVA glue
Battery-powered lights or tea lights and matches/a lighter

How to do it

1. Rinse your jar in warm soapy water to clean it out and remove any labels that might be stuck to the sides.
2. Collect some colourful leaves from the ground or a tree. Try to pick some that aren't completely dry as it will be easier to mould them to the jar.
3. Glue the leaves onto the sides of the jar. It doesn't matter too much if some sections overlap.
4. Drop in a battery-powered tea light or a real one. If the jar's too deep and you're struggling to light a real candle, then use a stick of spaghetti. It's super long and burns just enough to light a candlewick.

PUMPKIN VASES

When I first saw these pumpkin vases, I was blown away. The autumnal colour of the pumpkin works so well with any seasonal flower arrangement and it will fill the room with a subtle pumpkin smell too. The best thing is just as the pumpkin starts to turn bad, you can carve it for Halloween. It's the craft that keeps on crafting!

You will need
A sharp kitchen knife
A pumpkin
A large spoon or ice-cream scoop
Flowers (plastic ones work best)

How to do it

1. Using your knife, slice a round hole in the top of your pumpkin.
2. Scoop out the insides with your spoon or ice-cream scoop and use for some tasty pumpkin recipes — it makes great soup!
3. Give the hollowed pumpkin shell a rinse or two to make sure you remove any stray pieces left behind.
4. Place some flowers inside and add a splash of water (if they're real).
5. Check on your pumpkin vase every day and when it starts looking a bit worse for wear, just empty the shell and get carving for Halloween.

PINE-CONE FUZZY FELT FOXES

I'm absolutely in love with these fuzzy foxes. They're so cute and small and you can hide them around your house for your kids to find. Does he hide snacks? Does he hide the TV remote? Who knows what that cheeky little fox will get up to but he'll definitely provide hours of fun.

You will need
A pine cone
Coloured felt
A pen
Scissors
Glue stick
Googly eyes

How to do it
1. Lay a pine cone on to your felt and trace a shape onto the felt so it fits your pine cone.

2. Cut out the shape and then create more foxy details with other colours, such as ears and a big bushy tail.

3. Glue the pieces of felt together, add the googly eyes, then leave to dry. Once dry, glue them to the pine cone.

HOMEMADE STICK ART

Get your own bespoke home accessory for the price of some glue and a can of spray paint. This gorgeous stick creation can be hung from picture hooks, sit on your mantelpiece or decorate the garden.

You will need
A bundle of sticks
2 large sheets of cardboard
A pen
Scissors or a Stanley knife
Glue
Sheets of old newspaper
A can of spray paint
Hook or nail, for hanging
(optional)

How to do it
1. Gather a decent amount of sticks and twigs from your local park or your garden. Sticks that are a little bit bendy and pliable are ideal.
2. Draw any shape you wish to design on one sheet of cardboard then cut it out. Simple shapes, such as hearts or stars, work best.
3. Start placing the sticks out on the cardboard shape and use your glue to carefully stick them to each other.
4. Once you have your shape built up and stuck together, leave it to dry overnight.
5. Once it's dry, take the second sheet of cardboard and in a well-ventilated area and on a few sheets of old newspaper, cover the twigs with your spray paint and leave it to dry.
6. Due to the nature of your stick creation, it should be easy to hang it directly onto a wall using a hook or nail. Or it will also look great placed on a mantelpiece or shelf.

HOMEMADE PLAY-DOH

This homemade version of Play-Doh costs practically nothing to make and provides hours of fun. It takes less than five minutes to make and the kids can help out too.

You will need
640ml warm water
4 small bowls and 1 large bowl
4 different colours of food colouring
Lemon juice, vegetable or coconut oil
1kg plain flour, plus extra for dusting
400g table salt
Chopping board (optional)

How to do it
1. Get your warm water, room temperature should be fine, and add 160ml to each of your 4, small bowls.
2. Add a few drops of food colouring to each bowl, using a different colour in each bowl.
3. Add ½ a tablespoon of either lemon juice, vegetable oil or coconut oil to each bowl. This will help to preserve the dough and also make it more pliable. I prefer using lemon juice as it's less greasy than the oil and makes the dough smell really nice.
4. Put the flour and salt into the large bowl and mix them together with your hands.
5. Evenly distribute the flour and salt mixture between the 4 bowls and mix together.
6. When the mixture in each bowl has formed one large lump, sprinkle a chopping board or a flat surface with flour and knead each ball of dough until it's soft and smooth.
7. Then it's ready to mould into whatever creations you and the kids can come up with. The dough should last up to 10 days if you keep it in a cupboard in a sealed plastic container or resealable sandwich bag when you're not using it.

DIY LAVA LAMP

I LOVED lava lamps as a kid and if I'd known about this homemade version, I would have filled my entire room with them. It's amazing entertainment and a funky decoration all in one.

You will need
A tall glass or bottle
Water
Food colouring
Vegetable or sunflower oil
An indigestion tablet containing sodium bicarbonate (I used an Alka-Seltzer tablet)

How to do it
1. Fill one-third of your bottle with tap water.
2. Add a few drops of food colouring to tint the water.
3. Fill the rest of the bottle with the oil.
4. Add an indigestion tablet and watch it go!

for the kids. You'll find nine times out of ten they'll be relieved too. We have this rule with our wider family, and it saves everyone a lot of time and money.

4. Do secret Santa

If you still want the adults to get a present too, then why not do a family secret Santa? Everyone pulls a name out of a hat and you only buy for that person. Set a limit on how much everyone has to spend — £10 or £20 normally works well.

5. Make your own gift sets

Don't buy gift sets of toiletries as you'll pay a premium for them. Have a go at making your own instead. Poundland sell hamper kits for £1 that include cellophane, tissue paper and tags or pick up some baskets at B&M. Throughout the year, I check the clearance section at Boots and buy discounted toiletries and beauty products. The Primark beauty section is great too for reduced bath bombs and face masks. I'll also save any free beauty samples that I get as well as miniatures from hotels. I put everything into a plastic storage container that I keep in my stockpile then when it gets to Christmas, I have a good selection of stuff to make some beauty hampers for people. It saves money and it's much more personal than a shop-bought gift set. I also do other themed hampers for close family. I do food ones for my brother and for my dad I'll put in some of his favourite bars of chocolate and a bottle of the cider that he loves.

6. Make your own digital Christmas cards

Many people don't send paper Christmas cards any more. It's much cheaper and more convenient to send a digital one. We take a family photo of us all in our Christmas pyjamas then I make an ecard out of it and print a few off to send to older

relatives. You could just email it out as a photo and put a
Merry Christmas banner on it. It's more personal than a
shop-bought Christmas card and people like to keep it
because it's a photo too.

7. Try some retro Christmas crafts

If you do receive cards, then after Christmas, cut out the
design on the front to make gift tags for the following year.
This is something I used to do with my parents as a kid, and
my girls enjoy doing it too. Retro craft ideas like this are back
in fashion and they're a good way to reuse and recycle
things. You could also try making paper chains out of
coloured scrap paper.

8. Set up a separate savings account for Christmas

Modern banking apps like Monzo give you a hand with
budgeting and let you set your money aside in 'pots'. You can
either put money aside each month for Christmas or it will
automatically skim money from your bank account and put
it in a savings pot of your choice.

9. Book your Christmas travel early

If you're planning to travel via train for Christmas don't
wait until the last minute to book tickets as they hike up
the price. Always try to book at least three months in
advance. With flights, it's best to book a year before
you're due to fly to get the cheapest seats during the
festive season.

10. Join a Christmas savings scheme

Christmas savings schemes like Park (getpark.co.uk) are
worth doing if you don't think you have the willpower to put

money away yourself or you're worried that you'll dip into it. You set an amount to save and each week they will take it out of your bank account by direct debit. When it gets close to Christmas, you can use the money you've saved to buy hampers, gifts and vouchers. I would recommend just sticking to the gift vouchers because everything else is more expensive than you'd pay on the high street. You can buy combined vouchers split between Tesco and Love2Shop, which you can use in over 300 different stores. You can use them to shop for Christmas or give them to people as presents. Every year I get a book of vouchers and if there's someone I haven't got a present for in my stockpile, I'll give them a voucher.

WHAT TO BUY IN THE JANUARY SALES TO SAVE YOU CASH NEXT CHRISTMAS

After Christmas, the high-street stores and supermarkets need to get rid of all their festive stock so everything goes into clearance. Things are reduced in stages — at the beginning of January everything is 50% off and by the end of the month, you can often get up to 90% off. So, if you can, hang on for the best deals.

Crackers, decorations and wrapping paper

I buy everything that I need for the following Christmas in the January sales. It's the best time to buy decorations, crackers and wrapping paper and I never pay full price for these items. In Asda's sale I picked up a luxury Christmas tree for £2, premium crackers reduced from £15 to £2 a box and wrapping paper for 5p a roll. I store them all in the loft with my Christmas decorations and bring them down on 1st December. I like to leave the reduced stickers on everything as I get such a rush from seeing all of the bargains.

Matching family pyjamas

For the last few years in the UK, matching Christmas pyjamas have been a huge trend and each retailer does their own version. I absolutely love it, but it can be expensive buying five pairs. I only buy ours in the January sales when they're reduced. This year we've got Disney-themed ones from Asda that were down from £15 per pair to £2. Just remember to get the size your kids are going to be in next Christmas. Pyjamas also make great Christmas presents, so if you see a good bargain, stock up and give them as gifts the following year.

Christmas outfits for kids

I love dressing my kids in Christmas-themed outfits, but they can be expensive, so I buy them in the January sales. Every year most schools have a Christmas jumper day, so I always get the girls theirs in the sales. If you've got a baby or a toddler, then the sales are the time to buy Christmas-themed outfits and sleepsuits. Just remember to buy the right size. I got £350 worth of Christmas clothes for Cloud for £35 in the January sale at Next.

WHEN TO BUY TO GET THE BEST BARGAINS

When it comes to Christmas, forward planning saves you money. There are certain times of year when things go on sale that will allow you to buy ahead. Many of these items can be put in your stockpile and used as presents or saved for the following Christmas.

JANUARY

The best time to buy Christmas decorations, crackers, cards and wrapping paper.

FEBRUARY/MARCH

Chocolate – the best time to get reduced chocolate is after Valentine's Day and Easter. Boxes of chocolates reduced after 14 February will often have up to a year on their expiry date so you could put them away for Christmas. Chocolate eggs can be reduced to as little as 10p after Easter, but they generally have a shorter expiry date so they're good to buy to use for baking or just to eat.

Craft supplies – after Easter there are always discounts on spring craft supplies. Hobbycraft always do a big sale at this time of year.

AUGUST

This is when outdoor toys like bouncy castles and paddling pools tend to go on sale. Items like BBQs, garden furniture and inflatable hot tubs take up a lot of room in the supermarkets and stores, so they need to clear them to make space for autumn stock.

SEPTEMBER

Stationery is always cheapest in September after the kids have gone back to school. Stock up on discounted pens, pencils, pencil cases and notebooks so you can make a nice bundle to give to people for birthdays or Christmas.

NOVEMBER

Fancy dress costumes are always reduced after Halloween. Not all of them are scary so you could buy a Disney princess dress or a superhero costume that would work for a birthday or Christmas present.

Festive hacks

Remember to **stock up on batteries** before Christmas. I've been caught out on Christmas Day before and haven't had any batteries for the girls' new toys, and they cost a fortune in corner shops or petrol stations. Now I make sure that I always have a couple of packs of batteries in every size in my stockpile. I get mine from Poundland.

Buy expensive toy advent calendars in the sale and put them away for the following year. On 1st December all the advent calendars get reduced and you can pick up a branded toy one like LEGO® or Playmobil for a couple of pounds when they were £20 or more. You can always use the contents for your wooden reusable advent calendar or if you don't want to wait until Christmas, you can use the toys in party bags.

Festive wrapping paper doesn't only have to be used at Christmas. Some of the designs I bought in the January sale at Asda, such as metallic leopard print and rainbow coloured stars, can be used for birthdays too. At 5p a roll, it was well worth me stocking up.

I have a family tradition where every Christmas Eve I go to the M&S food hall to **buy the turkey**. I get there an hour before it closes and head for the meat section. My local store is not as busy as some supermarkets that can be packed on Christmas Eve and they usually reduce like crazy! Every single year I've saved money on fresh meat and veg – my best bargain was a turkey reduced from £40 to 50p!! We always have Christmas dinner at a massively discounted price.

EXPERT HACKS!

Thank you to money-saving blogger **Francesca (themoneyfox.com)** for this one:

I get a lot of my daughter's presents from car boot sales. There are a lot of brand-new toys and books at car boots and even if the things are second hand they're generally in excellent condition and she doesn't mind whether they're in their packaging or not.

When it comes to saving at Christmas, my friend and blogger **Donna (savvymumuk.co.uk)** knows a thing or two:

Pay money into your Amazon account every time you can. I put £7 a week away and don't touch it until Christmas so I've built up a nice amount to help with gifts.

Do you really need to buy presents? Every year I struggle to know what to buy for my father. It gets harder and harder for me to buy for him to the point where I always end up getting him something that he doesn't really need. Why not consider making a donation to a charity in their name instead?

AMAZING MEMBERS' HACKS

'Every Christmas I take my kids to see the Coca-Cola Truck. They release locations a few months before Christmas, so you can plan your visit, and you get a free mini can of Coke each and a lovely photo in front of the truck. The best thing is it's free.'

'Every month buy a gift card from a store that you shop at during the Christmas period and put it away for Christmas.'

'Get a Christmas Money Saving Tin (one you have to open with a can opener!) to stop you dipping in. Every month myself and my wife put in £10 each and by Christmas we have £240 to spend.'

'Some local butchers have Christmas schemes which you can pay into each month. Then in December you use the balance to pay for your turkey and trimmings. It's a great way to get quality meat and support a local business.'

'I save with a credit union all year round. There's loads of Unions to choose from and even one for NHS.'

... Throw a cheap kid's birthday party

The average children's birthday party now costs £320 but you don't have to spend anywhere near that much to give your little one a fantastic day. So, here are my top ten money-saving tips on how to have a party on a budget.

MY TOP TEN TIPS TO THROW A KID'S PARTY ON A BUDGET

1. Have a party at home

When I was little, my mum wouldn't dream of spending hundreds of pounds on a party and all of mine were held at home. Keep it simple and play some traditional games like pass the parcel, musical statues and sleeping lions. If the children are older then get some craft kits for them to do, such as paint a mug or decorate a wooden jewellery box (you can get some cheap craft kits from Poundland, Home Bargains and B&M). They can take home what they've made at the party, so it saves you buying party bags too.

2. Hire a church or community hall

This is a great option if you're inviting the whole class as it works out quite cheaply. Our local village hall is £12 an hour. We hire it for three hours — half an hour to set up, a two-hour party and half an hour to clean up at the end. We hire a bouncy castle and bring our own food. The kids love it and there's plenty of space so they can run around and let off steam.

3. Offer a choice

Don't always assume that your child wants a big party — some kids may find it really stressful to be the centre of attention. I certainly wasn't a fan of big parties as a child. Offer them a choice instead. Ask them if they'd prefer a party or to go on a family day out to their favourite theme park or maybe a zoo or safari park. If you use vouchers, a day out can work out a lot cheaper than a party and the whole family gets a treat as well.

4. Party in the park

If your child has a spring or summer birthday, then head to your local park for a picnic. Buy some cheap outdoor games from Poundland or organise some races — things like a three-legged or egg and spoon race always go down well. For preschoolers, you could make it into a teddy bear's picnic. Buy some cardboard boxes on eBay and make each child their own lunchbox — pop in a sandwich, some crisps, a box of juice and a sweet treat and you're good to go (after checking with other parents for allergies). It's so simple to do and works out to be really inexpensive. Bring or borrow a gazebo on the day just in case it rains.

5. Don't get a package and go off-peak

It can cost up to £16 per child or more to have a party package at a soft play area, trampoline park or bowling alley. In some venues, you're paying for exclusive hire and even if you're not you're paying a premium for food (which to be honest isn't normally the best quality). The cost soon mounts up if you're inviting lots of guests and you're paying for convenience. Instead, don't book the expensive party package. The kids aren't bothered about having the whole place to themselves or a private party room. Just book them in on a normal slot and take your own food and drink if you're allowed.

Another money-saving option is to have the party outside of a weekend — great for kids not yet at school. Organise it at an off-peak time, such as after school, when admission will be a lot cheaper. Many of these places have off-peak deals.

6. Watch a movie

Take advantage of the cheap screenings at your local cinema and take a group of kids for a party. Odeon do kids' screenings on Saturday and Sunday mornings for £2.50 a child and adults go free when you buy a child's ticket. Afterwards you could take them to McDonald's for a Happy Meal. Kids love watching a movie with their friends and it's a very affordable party.

7. Have a joint party

If any of your children's friends or classmates have birthdays around the same time as them, then suggest having a joint party. Chances are they'd be inviting the same kids to come along and it will save on costs if you're splitting everything with another family.

8. Order pizza

So much food goes to waste at parties. Kids are too busy running around and having fun with their friends to sit and eat anything much. So, what we do is get takeaway pizzas. On the day of the party, we order Papa John's or Pizza Hut using a 50% off code (which you can easily find with a quick Google search). The pizzas are delivered to the venue, we lay them out on a big table in their boxes and everyone can grab a slice. They cater for vegans and allergies and intolerances too. I've found that if you get pizza, it always gets eaten and you can just recycle the boxes afterwards so it's quick and easy to clean up. If the kids don't eat them, the parents will!

9. Check out your local sports centre

If you're planning a party, then have a look at what your local sports centre offers. They often have all sorts of parties from football and soft play to trampolining and are normally quite reasonably priced. Swimming parties can work out to be inexpensive too — you can get exclusive hire of a pool from around £60–70 and they'll often throw in floats and inflatables. You'll normally get a room afterwards included in the price so you can bring your own food. Or some sports centres offer a roller-skating party. Play some music through a speaker, those kids that have skates can bring them or the sports centre will have skates that you can hire.

10. Have a sleepover or a camp out

Kids absolutely love a sleepover or a camping party. Pitch a tent in your garden and camp out (with an adult to supervise) overnight. Have a barbecue and toast marshmallows before settling the kids down in their sleeping bags for the night. Or if it's not warm enough to camp, have a sleepover. Everyone brings a sleeping bag and an inflatable mattress or travel bed and they can watch a movie in their PJs and have a midnight feast (but slightly earlier than midnight!). These sorts of parties work well for older children (eight or nine plus I'd say) and a smaller group. They're very inexpensive to do but be warned, you might not get much sleep!

MONEY-SAVING PARTY BAG AND PRESENT IDEAS

Buy birthday presents in advance

My daughters have thirty kids in each of their classes and we have at least fifteen birthday parties to go to each year. If you leave it until the last minute to buy a child's birthday present, then you end up spending a fortune.

Like Christmas, forward planning for birthday parties will save you money. If I see a good bargain throughout the year, I'll buy it and put it in my stockpile. Then if one of my girls comes home with an invite from seven-year-old Daniel, I know I'll have something suitable. I also have lots of birthday cards and wrapping paper in my stockpile too.

What to buy and where

Poundland is great for books. Often the Guinness Book of World Records will end up in there after Christmas and kids tend to love those. Look out for popular brands like LEGO®, Play-Doh and Playmobil that are heavily reduced in Home Bargains and B&M as they always seem to go down well with most children.

Make a hamper

When I first started stockpiling, *Frozen* had just come out and all the kids were obsessed by it. So, I went to Poundland and bought five *Frozen*-themed items. Then I bought a nice box and some tissue paper and made a hamper out of them. You can do this with stationery and toiletries too.

Theme your present

We have a local play area near us that's pirate-themed and it's always popular for birthday parties. Sometimes it's nice to tie the present in with the party theme, so whenever I see any pirate-themed items reduced, I'll buy them and put them in my stockpile. I've bought pirate bubble bath and stationery before and even a pirate costume. Princesses are another popular theme that always come in handy.

Buy ahead for cheap party bags

Plan ahead and stockpile items for party bags throughout the year. Look in the sales and if you see a good bargain, then buy several and keep them in your stockpile. Little toys, stationery and even books work well. I've picked up whole packets of Crayola crayons for 20p each before and chocolate surprise eggs with toys inside from Home Bargains for 19p each. If you see packets of sweets reduced to 5 or 10p then they're always worth buying and saving for party bags too — just check the best before dates.

If you haven't had a chance to stockpile, then go to Amazon or eBay where you can bulk buy party bag toys, such as 20 mini colouring books, for a few pounds. The supermarkets have party bag sections, but I wouldn't advise you buying them from there as they're a lot more expensive.

Holly's HACKS

Party hacks

Don't tell my kids, but **I've never paid full price for any of their birthday cakes**. At 8pm the night before one of my children's birthdays, I go to a couple of supermarkets and see what's reduced. I've never failed to buy a discounted birthday cake and I normally get them so cheap that I buy two or three. I've picked up animal-themed cakes, Disney

princesses and other character cakes all for around £1.50 each rather than the £12–20 that they normally cost, and my kids absolutely love them.

If your child has a summer birthday, then have **a garden party**. On a hot day, fill up a couple of padding pools (make sure there's an adult there to supervise them at all times) or let them have a water fight with water guns or pistols. Water bombs always go down a treat too. Make sure they come in their swimwear or have a spare pair of clothes.

Don't bother buying paper invitations. **Invite people by emailing or texting parents.** If you want to do an invite, then get your child to draw a picture or design their own then photocopy or scan it.

EXPERT HACKS!

Some great tips from money-saving blogger **Katy Stevens (katykicker.com)** – thanks Katy!

If your child's going to a party, ask the host if there's an Amazon wishlist that you can buy them a gift from. More parents are doing this and it's easier to buy something that you know the child wants and it stops them getting duplicate items.

Club together with a group of parents to purchase one large gift for the child whose birthday it is. Everyone makes a small contribution and the recipient gets a present they will truly appreciate.

When you're hosting a birthday party, avoid lunch or dinner time and instead have an array of snacks and treats. There will be less food wasted and it means you don't have to provide a full meal for the party guests.

AMAZING MEMBERS' HACKS

'For cheap bouncy castle hire look on Facebook marketplace — you can often get some good deals. Talk to your local takeaway and see if they'll do a pizza and chips bundle for a set amount.'

'I got a Monzo bank account and for every purchase it rounds up the change to the nearest pound and puts it into another account. I'm using it to save up for my son's first birthday party.'

'My local bowling alley does everything for half price on a Tuesday including laser tag, drinks and food so you'd save a lot if you had a party on that day.'

Random acts of kindness

One rainy afternoon a few years ago, I was struggling to find ways to entertain my girls Mollie and Bella. So, I decided to explain to them where their food comes from, how it grows in the fields and is picked and how it then goes to a factory. We went into our kitchen cupboards and looked at all the food we had and talked about how it had been made and which were our favourites and why.

• •

When we were looking at the labels, I noticed there was a freepost customer care address on all of them. I imagined someone sat in an office somewhere and I thought how nice it would be to write to them to say thank you for our food. I suspected that these people were normally the ones who got all the complaints.

I had a box of thank you cards in my stockpile that I'd picked up cheaply from The Works, so I wrote a little note saying how much we loved their brand and thanked them for their delicious food. The girls wanted to draw them a picture too and we then we posted them off to our favourite brands.

I didn't think any more of it until a few weeks later when we started receiving all these letters and packages back from the brands thanking the girls for their pictures and notes. I was blown away by all the lovely things they sent us from vouchers and money-off coupons to badges, balls and toys. We once got a £200 hamper from a sausage company and a photo of the pig farmer holding up Mollie and Bella's drawing which the girls absolutely loved.

It was a bit of a random idea and we honestly didn't expect anything in return, but it made me realise how we're so quick to give negative feedback to brands so it's nice for them to get positive feedback from happy customers as well.

HOW YOU CAN DO IT TOO

☺ Brands love feedback. They like hearing from customers who use their products and love them.

☺ Find your own unique way of approaching your favourite brands. If you really enjoy their products, then tell them.

☺ If you know a brand that you like is celebrating a significant birthday or anniversary (you'll often see this on the packaging) then why not send them a birthday or congratulations card?

☺ If you have a story involving a brand, then let them know. Perhaps you've called your dog after your favourite brand of chocolate bar or a certain ice cream has got you through a break-up with your boyfriend?

☺ Brands especially love funny stories. These always go down well as they can re-tweet them and they make great marketing. Or why not just tweet a brand your favourite joke? Twitter is a brilliant tool to connect you with your favourite manufacturers.

Don't do any of this expecting to be sent free things. Yes, it's nice and you might receive a coupon, a gift voucher or one of their products through the post, but don't expect anything. Do it as a goodwill gesture and you never know, you might be pleasantly surprised.

Free things!

I've always had a passion for free stuff. When I was a kid, I used to go on freebie sites and order free samples for my entire family. I still love a freebie now. It's a good way to try new products and they're really handy to have in my stockpile or to give away to people. These offers are available to anyone so find out how you can also get something for nothing.

• •

Freebie websites

These are specialist websites that list all the freebies currently available. They're free to join and you get a newsletter alerting you to the manufacturers that are currently giving things away. Some of the biggest ones are magicfreebies.co.uk and freesamples.co.uk and they often have a corresponding Facebook group where members share information about freebies they've found, so they're well worth joining.

Sending out freebies is a great marketing tool for brands, especially if they're launching a new product. Many companies do this rather than investing in big advertising campaigns and it's a way of getting feedback. By giving you a free sample, companies are potentially getting your custom and if you like it, you'll probably tell your friends about it. A lot of freebies are household cleaning products and toiletries. I've had dishwasher tablets and washing powder, plus personalised razors from Wilkinson Sword worth £10 each.

Tena Lady always offer great freebies where they'll give you a whole pack worth £8, which I'll claim and then donate to my local care home. Miniature toiletries are always useful when you're going away for a weekend and you don't want to take a full-sized bottle with you.

One word of warning — be mindful if you're applying for a freebie and you're being asked for lots of details, such as your date of birth, your household income and if you're a homeowner. These are likely to be market research companies trying to collect your data to sell on. You won't get a guaranteed freebie either, you'll just be put in a draw to win one and they're best avoided. Go for the genuine freebies where a well-known brand or company is giving a product away for you to try.

Freebies with magazines

Always browse the magazine section in the shops as some come with freebies that are a higher value than the magazine itself. Glossy monthly mags, such as *Cosmopolitan* and *Red*, regularly have high-end make-up and skincare freebies. It's also worth looking at craft magazines for free craft kits.

Reach out to brands

If you're expecting a baby or getting married, then why not contact relevant brands and ask them for free samples? You can write to them via email, post or by messaging them on social media. As you'll have read earlier (see page 59), I've had huge success with this.

Rewards from your mobile phone

It's definitely worth joining the reward programmes that come with your mobile phone. One of the biggest ones is O2

Priority where if you download the app you can get everything from a free snack or drink with your lunch and the chance to win a car or a holiday to priority pre-sale tickets and perks at O2 venues. EE customers can currently get a free three-month subscription to the BT Sports app and other freebies and discounts and the Vodafone VeryMe rewards app offers freebies from Costa Coffee, Millie's Cookies and Hotel Chocolat. The freebies on offer change weekly so it's worth downloading the app and checking with your provider.

Freebies on your birthday

I once worked out that on average, you can get around £100 worth of free stuff from brands on your birthday if you're signed up to their loyalty schemes or apps. These are just a selection of some of the things that you can claim:

- ☺ **A free meal.** Many restaurants will offer you a free main meal including Beefeater, Frankie & Benny's and Brewers Fayre.
- ☺ **Free sweet treats.** You can claim a free cake, donut or sweet treat at Greggs. A free donut at Krispy Kreme and free cookies at Subway and Millie's Cookies.
- ☺ **Free drinks.** Some bars and restaurants will offer you a free cocktail or drink on your birthday including a free bottle of prosecco at Pizza Express and a complimentary milkshake at Ed's Diner.
- ☺ **Free vouchers.** Many stores will send you a free £5 voucher on your birthday if you're a member of their loyalty or reward schemes including Paperchase, The Body Shop, Smiggle and Hobbycraft.

And your pet doesn't need to miss out either. Pets at Home will give them a free treat if you take them into one of their stores on their birthday.

Free food and drink

It's well worth downloading the apps for your favourite restaurant chains, takeaways, pubs and bars as you'll often get free food and drinks as an introductory offer. McDonald's will give you a free cheeseburger when you download their app, Greggs offer a free sausage roll and KFC will give you a complimentary side. Some pub chains will give you a free drink if you download their app including All Bar One, Sizzling Pubs, Miller & Carter and Browns. I've even read stories about students doing a whole pub crawl by claiming their free drinks in various bars!

FREE SOFTWARE

With more people than ever working from home, make the most of what's available without having to pay a penny. The only downside is a lot of free versions are ad-supported (so you will get the odd advert pop up here and there) but to me, that's only a small inconvenience considering the money you're saving.

Free antivirus software

To protect your laptop or PC, you need an antivirus programme. Free programmes include:

Avast — avast.com (Windows, Mac and Android)
Avira — avira.com (Windows and Mac)
AVG Antivirus — avg.com (Windows, Mac and Android)
Bitdefender — bitdefender.com (Windows, Mac and Android)
Malwarebytes — malwarebytes.com

Free office software

Here's six of the best:

FreeOffice — freeoffice.com/en — Similar to Microsoft Office and the basic functions are free.

Google Docs — google.co.uk/docs/about/ — One of the best free office applications.

LibreOffice — libreoffice.org — Good if you need to do graphs and diagrams as part of your work.

Microsoft Office Online — office.com — Make sure you select Office Online from the 'products' section as you have to pay for some products.

Polaris Office — polarisoffice.com/en — Includes everything you need to create and edit documents, presentations and spreadsheets.

WPS — wps.com/ — integrates Word, PDFs, Excel, PowerPoint, Forms, as well as Cloud Storage, Template Gallery and Online Editing & Sharing.

Free photo editing software

To add effects to your photos, you need photo editing software. Why not try these free resources?

Canva — canva.com/ — A browser-based graphic design platform. Good for creating posters, banners and flyers or images for social media. Features lots of easy to use templates.

Fotor — fotor.com — Features simple tools that will help you crop photos, resize images, add effects, text and filters.

GIMP — www.gimp.org — A cross-platform image editor. Good all-rounder.

Gravit Designer — gravit.io — This is the tool I use and recommend. Ideal for creating layouts.

Pixlr — pixlr.com — Helps you add layers and effects to images and has a lot of the features that you normally see in desktop graphic design applications.

More free hacks!

Borrow free ebooks, audiobooks and magazines from your library using your phone or tablet. Go to overdrive.com and use your local library card to search their collection. You can borrow (download) anything they have to offer, and the great thing is they 'auto return' once your loan expires.

If you're aged between thirteen and twenty-four you can **register for the NHS c-card scheme** to get free condoms, Femidoms, lube, dams and information and advice on contraception and STIs. Go to icash.nhs.uk for more information.

If you're a **student,** then it's worth getting a TOTUM card. It's £14.99 for a year's membership but if you pay for two years then you'll get an additional year for free. It gives you access to hundreds of freebies as well as savings in shops, restaurants and websites. Go to totum.com for more info.

EXPERT HACKS TO FIND THE BEST FREEBIES!

Top tips from **Tom Bryant**, founder of **www.magicfreebiesuk. co.uk** — the biggest freebie site in the UK:

- ☺ **Become a product tester.** Certain companies want people to sit on their panels whereby you get sent free products to test out and give your feedback on. You register on their website and if you're in the right demographic for that particular product, they'll email you and invite you to take part. One of the biggest is Savvy Circle run by Procter & Gamble. You can sign up on their website (supersavvyme.co.uk) to become a Savvy Circle ambassador and try out new P&G products. For example, they recently wanted 2,000 people to test out a Flash Powermop. Philips also run a popular product testing scheme for their electronic items. You sign up on their website (producttester.philips.com) and apply for the tests that you're interested in. Boots also have a testing site — bootsvolunteers.com. The more reviews you do and the more thorough you are with your feedback, the more likely these panels are to use you again.

- ☺ **Join an online bank.** New online banking apps, such as Chip, Curve and Starling, will give you free money for joining and they'll give you cash for referring friends too. It's usually anything between £5 and £20. Some members of our Facebook group have earned hundreds of pounds worth of referrals.

- ☺ **Like a brand's Facebook page.** Certain brands give freebies away on Facebook to people who like their page.

It tends to be cosmetics and once you like their page, you'll start getting adverts for free samples of their new products in your Facebook feed. Companies that do this include Armani and YSL, John Frieda, Rituals and Sanctuary Spa. They send you an email with an authentication code that you type into a website. It's well worth doing as often it's a travel-sized shower gel, hair product, tube of foundation or a small lipstick and not just a one-use sachet.

☺ **Get a free subscription box.** There are so many subscription services available now and many of them will offer you the first box for free when you join – you just have to pay for postage. Graze.com will give you your first snack box for free and Beer52.com will send you your first box of craft beer for free. It contains eight beers, a magazine and a snack and you just have to pay the postage. Many razor companies, such as Gillette and Harry's, do a subscription service where your starter kit is free. When you join the Tails.com dog food subscription you'll get a free two-week dog food bag by just paying £1 for postage. Always read the terms and conditions before you join a subscription service to check that you can cancel at any time and are not tied in for a set period. Then set a Google calendar alert to remind you to cancel the subscription after your first free box if you don't want to continue.

☺ **Get a free journey.** Check out apps, such as Uber and Bolt, as you'll often get your first ride for free. You'll also get extra credit for referring a friend.

AMAZING MEMBERS' HACKS

'I use Send Me a Sample. You register for an account then look out for the Send Me a Sample logo next to products online. If you see it, just ask your Alexa or Google device to 'Send you a Sample' then it's delivered direct to your door.'

'Download the hotukdeals app. There's a freebie section that is updated whenever a new freebie is available.'

'Use free online storage providers, such as Google Drive and Microsoft Drive, to store all your photos, files and documents instead of spending money on external hard drives.'

MAKING MØNEY

→ I didn't want this book just to be about saving money. Over the years, I've come up with easy, quick and achievable ways to make money too. They're all things that I do to make myself a bit of extra cash. So, whether that's using your smartphone to make money for a holiday, selling some items in your house that you didn't realise were worth anything or starting a career as a mystery shopper, I've got the advice for you.

Money for nothing

Reselling things that you already own is a great way to make some extra cash. So many of us have items lying around at home that perhaps we don't even realise are worth anything. Find out how you can turn your clutter into cash.

• •

THINGS YOU MIGHT NOT REALISE ARE WORTH SELLING

Empty toilet paper rolls

Don't throw the cardboard tubes away when the loo roll has finished – you could be making money from them instead. Some savvy people sell boxes of loo rolls on sites like eBay or Gumtree. A box of fifty could sell for around £5 and a hundred for £10. People use them for school projects, all sorts of arts and crafts and for protecting plants and seeds. I'm currently saving mine up to sell!

TV remote controls

Did you know that old TV remote controls could be worth something? If they're from a brand like Samsung or Panasonic and they're from a model of TV that is no longer being sold, then it could be worth selling them on eBay. People constantly lose or break remotes but if they have to replace them for an older model then they'll have to go

For Winter

If there was ever a season when you needed to save money, then Christmas is the one. These crafts will not only save cash but they make sweet, original surprises for your friends and family.

BOOK ADVENT CALENDAR

This advent calendar is a lovely alternative to a chocolate one.
You can often pick up sets of books cheaply at the bargain stores
(you could collect them throughout the year to spread the cost)
and it's nice to get some Christmassy reads in there to get you in
the festive mood.

You will need
24 books (buy them cheaply from
Poundland or The Works)
Wrapping paper
Scissors
Tape
Ribbon
A present bow (optional)
Label
Pen

How to do it
1. Buy 24 books. Pick the books
    according to your child's age
    and reading ability. It's a nice
    touch if some of the books are
    Christmas-themed.
2. Wrap the books separately and
    then stack them into a pile. I'd
    recommend sorting them by size
    so that they look better — largest
    at the bottom and smallest
    at the top.
3. Simply tie them together with
    some ribbon, add a bow on the top
    if you like and then a small label
    explaining that this is your child's
    advent calendar and that they can
    open one of the parcels every day.

THE VERY MERRY CHOCOLATE WREATH

What could be more fun and festive? An unusual wreath that not only looks quirky but that you can eat too!

You will need
Foam wreath (available from craft shops or florists)
Double-sided sticky tape or glue dots
Packets of fun-size sweets and/or chocolate bars
Ribbon for hanging (optional)

How to do it

1. Grab your foam wreath and roughly measure how many sweets it will take to cover the surface of it. This will help make the finished project look much nicer.
2. Place strips of double-sided sticky tape or glue dots around the foam ring so that the sweets have a good base to stick to.
3. Add your fun-size sweets to the sticky sections of the wreath.

Try to glue them in the middle of the sweets so the ends are still accessible. When it comes to eating them later, you want to make sure you can still open the wrappers.

Top tip: Work in a circular pattern rather than just sticking them on randomly. A colour-coordinated or pattern effect will give your wreath the wow factor.

4. Try your absolute best not to eat your materials while you work! As long as the seals on the packets aren't damaged or open then your treats should still be fine to eat after Christmas. But will you be able to wait until the festivities are over before you tuck in?
5. Add a ribbon bow and use it to hang the wreath on a wall, if you like.

BEAUTIFUL BUDGET PAPER PRESENTS

When one of my Facebook members said they'd wrapped all their Christmas gifts in newspaper, I must admit I was a bit sceptical at first. But when I saw how incredible the finished presents looked under the tree, I was an instant convert. I might still use shop-bought wrapping paper for the kids, but the adults are always getting these beautiful vintage-looking gifts.

You will need
Old newspaper
Iron
Scissors
Sellotape
Rustic string

How to do it

1. Find some old newspaper. For the best results, use the crossword section (unfinished of course!) or large sections of text. Black and white paper with no pictures is the top choice.

2. Using an iron on the LOWEST temperature setting, iron out the paper so it's perfectly crisp and flat.

3. Wrap your presents as you normally would — or if you're like me, get someone to do it for you who can make it look really nice (thanks Callum!).

4. Finish the look with some rustic string that you can find in most Post Offices, stationery stores or craft shops.

CANDY-CANE SLEIGH

I'm always impressed when I see one of these. Not only can it make a fun little present for a secret Santa, you can also use these as decorations around the house or even on your tree . . . if you're clever enough to balance them on the branches that is!

You will need
Candy canes (minimum 2 per sleigh)
Glue stick
1 large, flat chocolate bar
A bundle of chocolates or sweet treats
Ribbon
Small chocolate Santa
Double-sided sticky tape

How to do it

1. Glue 2 candy canes to either side of the bottom of a large flat chocolate bar (KitKats work best). This is going to be your sleigh base.

2. Neatly stack the chocolates or sweet treats (largest on the bottom) on top of the sleigh base.

3. Using a length of ribbon, tie a bow around the sleigh and its contents. You might want to do a single or double loop of ribbon to keep everything secure.

4. Man the sleigh with a small chocolate Santa (Lindt and Kinder prove most popular with group members) and using a strip of double-sided sticky tape, secure it to the front of the sleigh.

THE CRAFTY HOME-MADE CALENDAR

This DIY *Christmas tree advent calendar brings a personal touch to the festive season and you can fill the tubes with anything you like.*

You will need

1 large piece of cardboard (the thicker the better)

24 toilet roll tubes or 12 kitchen roll tubes, cut in half

Gold or silver spray paint (optional)

Glue dots

24 goodies, such as small toys or sweets, to fill the tubes

Scissors

Card, foil, tissue paper or cloth

Pens

24 elastic bands

How to do it

1. Grab a large base sheet of cardboard (or any other suitable base to use for this), decorate it and arrange your 24 tubes into any Christmas shape you like. We chose a tree, but you could make a snowman or a present.

2. To make it look extra snazzy, spray paint the tubes and the base sheet silver or gold.

3. Using glue dots, stick the tubes to your base. If you're struggling to stick the tubes down, make 4 small cuts with a pair of scissors (about 1cm long) and fold to create flaps that can give you a sturdier hold.

4. Fill each tube with a small toy or sweet treat. If the calendar is for a child, then why not get one of Santa's elves to write a small note with a message about the Christmas spirit or to tell them that the elves are watching so they can let Santa know whether they've been naughty or nice!

5. Using card, foil, tissue paper or cloth, create 24 'doors' to cover the tubes. Decorate and number them from 1–24, then secure them to the tops of the tubes using the elastic bands.

directly to the manufacturer where they can pay up to £60.
My dad actually collects them, and he's got a box full that
he's picked up at car boot sales for a few pence.

Argos catalogues

I used to love the Argos catalogue as a kid, and old ones
always sell well on eBay. They're sought after by collectors as
they give a snapshot of a certain era that you can see through
all the items that were on sale. Catalogues from the 1970s
could make as much as £90 or more and ones from the
80s could make up to £60–70.

OTHER THINGS YOU CAN SELL ONLINE
TO MAKE MONEY

DVDs, books and computer games

If you have lots of DVDs, CDs, books and games to sell, there
are online companies that will buy them from you. Most of
them have apps with built-in barcode scanners that you use
to scan your items to find out how much they're worth. You
then package your items and send them to the company
using their pre-paid delivery service. Once they receive
them, you'll get paid either by bank transfer, Paypal or
cheque. Companies that do this are musicmagpie.co.uk,
ziffit.com and webuybooks.co.uk (they will also buy DVDs
and games).

At momox.co.uk you can sell vinyl records as well as CDs,
DVDs and games.

CeX stores buy DVDs, games and tech including laptops,
tablets, smart watches, games consoles and cameras. You can
do it online or in store. Go to uk.webuy.com for more details.

Things to look out for:

- ☺ Check your items before you send them and make sure they're in good condition. If DVDs or game discs are scratched, then they can refuse to accept them.
- ☺ Sign up to newsletters before selling your items as you'll often get a first-time seller offer giving you an extra percentage on the total of your items.
- ☺ Don't sell to the first site that you try. Download all the apps and sell to the one that offers you the most money.
- ☺ Use the apps to scan CDs, DVDs, games and books in charity shops and at car boots and you might find a real gem. I once bought a Nintendo GameCube game at a car boot sale for 50p and later scanned it to find I could trade it in for £15.

How much can you earn?

It all depends on how many items you have to sell. I recently sold a mix of twenty-two DVDs and computer games to Music Magpie and got £38.

HOW TO SELL YOUR OLD MOBILE PHONE FOR CASH

If you have an old phone you can sell it to a recycling website for cash. I often trade in my old phones once my contract is over and I normally get around £150. Sometimes they'll even take phones that are slightly damaged or not working although you'll get a lower price for it.

To sell your phone you type your phone's make, model and condition into the website, and they'll give you a price. If you accept it, they'll send you a pre-paid envelope or label so you can send your phone to them. Send the phone fully charged up, take out the sim card and restore factory settings so there are no security codes on it. Also remember to wipe out all the data and images. I'd also recommend taking a photo of it, so you have proof of its condition in case it gets damaged in the post.

How much is my old phone worth?

The recycling companies will check it to make sure it matches the details that you provided online. If it doesn't then they'll give you a new quote. How much you'll get depends on the model, what condition it's in, the network it's locked to and how old the phone is. They'll either resell it or break it down and sell the parts off.

Where can I sell my phone?

- ☺ If you've got a newer model of phone you could sell it yourself on eBay.
- ☺ Check how much you'd get for your phone by using a comparison site, such as comparemymobile.com, sellmymobile.com or compareandrecycle.co.uk.
- ☺ If you're not going to get much for it by selling it then trade it in when you're buying a new mobile and you could get a discount.
- ☺ Give it to charity. Most charities will accept old mobile phones that they resell to help raise funds.

EXPERT HACKS!

When it comes to knowing what's worth selling, my friend, **Joe Stutter,** is an expert. We met as teenagers on an auction website for kids called Swapitshop. He used to buy party toys and other small items that he would then split and sell individually for more points. He was an entrepreneur even at fifteen! He got a taste for it then and he's been buying and selling ever since. Here are Joe's hacks — thanks Joe!

How to find valuable items in your home

Your home could be full of treasures without you even realising it. Here are some of the items that sell really well and could earn you a bit of extra cash.

Food packaging

Old tins and jars advertising food brands can be worth something. Popular brands include Cadbury's, Jacob's Crackers and Ryvita. Enamel signs advertising fuel, such as Shell and Esso, also sell well. A lot of these retro items are used as props by interior designers and people like to display them in their own homes too.

One-off packaging collaborations can also be popular — Douwe Egberts released a coffee jar with an Orla Kiely design in 2013 and these now sell for around £10–15 each without the coffee inside. Not bad for an empty jar! So have a look in your kitchen cupboards and before you throw your granny's old biscuit tin away, do a quick search online to check that it's not worth something.

Books

Just because a book looks old, doesn't mean that it's worth anything unfortunately and most books lose their value over time. However, there are a few things worth looking out for. Check for:
- First editions
- Signed books
- Books with misprints or typos in them. I've sold a few Harry Potter books with typos in them — it makes them rarer because they're likely to have had a limited run.

☺ Books that have been made into TV shows or movies. The show or movie can reignite the book's popularity and people then want the original editions of the book.

DVDs

Most DVDs don't hold their original value, but you can sell them through buying companies, such as Music Magpie. If one of these companies offers you more than £2 for a DVD then this could indicate that it's worth something and you should definitely do some more research.

There are some DVDs that might hold their value and be worth selling individually:
☺ Box sets of TV shows that aren't on any streaming platforms
☺ Specialist documentaries and educational DVDs
☺ One-off DVDs that came free with newspapers
☺ Anime – computer animation that originates from Japan, such as Pokémon and Digimon. I've had some really good sales with anime DVDs with many of them fetching more than their original retail price.

Old video games and consoles

Lots of people collect old computer games and consoles so they're always in demand. Retro games always go down well – a bundle of old Tomb Raider games can sell for around £50 and old PlayStation games (especially if they're still sealed and have never been played) are sought after by collectors. I once sold a sealed PC game called Doom from 1994 for nearly £300. I've kept my old computer games from when I was a kid because I know they'll be worth something one day.

Action figures

Get out your old toys from the loft because collectors are always looking for action figures and if they're in their original packaging they can sell for hundreds of pounds. Popular figures are Star Wars, Transformers and cartoons from the 80s and 90s like Teenage Mutant Ninja Turtles and Thundercats. There are action figure identification groups on Facebook so you can tell which characters they are if you're not sure. Many figures will have the toy company brand and the date they were made on their back or leg.

LEGO®

The LEGO® sets that are worth the most are the ones that came out before 2000 from the original-style vintage LEGO® to 80s and 90s' collections, such as pirates, Halloween and space. If it's from a discontinued set and is still in a sealed box it's likely to be worth something. Even if you don't have a full set, a few bricks from a specific set can still be worth selling. Ornate pieces and bricks with words on are always worth looking out for as are the bricks from Harry Potter sets as the colours are different to every other LEGO® set. You can sell individual pieces on sites, such as bricklink.com.

Board games

Have a look through your cupboards and dig out your old board games. MB Board Games from the 80s and 90s like Mouse Trap and Ghost Castle can sell for up to £20—30 on eBay. Role-playing games such as Warhammer and Dungeon & Dragons will also sell — I once sold a 2003 Dungeons & Dragons game for £43. Vintage chess sets are also popular.

If you've got a few spare pieces for a game, they could be worth selling on eBay as people lose bits of games and want to replace them.

Polly Pocket/Bluebird Toys

Have you got a Big Yellow Teapot or a Big Red Bus toy gathering dust in the loft? The original series of Polly Pocket was made by Swindon company, Bluebird Toys in the early 90s and is sought after by collectors across the world with some complete play sets fetching hundreds of pounds. The range that the company did with Disney and Mattel called the Disney Tiny Collection also sells really well. I once sold a small figure and one piece, which I'd picked out of a bag of toys at a car boot, for £35. It tends to be the figures that are worth the most money and most products should say the original date on their base. The Mighty Max Range that was made by the same company is also very popular.

Soft toys

Often teddy bears and soft toys get chucked away or given to charity shops when kids get older. Most of them are mass-produced and aren't worth anything but there are a few exceptions.

Retro TV characters

Characters from classic shows, such as *Sesame Street*, *The Muppets*, *Rosie & Jim*, *ALF*, *Care Bears*, *Tots TV* and *The Sooty Show*, are always in demand. Anything that people reminisce about from their childhoods tends to sell. It's also worth looking out for TV mascots like Basil Brush, Gordon the Gopher and more modern characters, such as Nev the bear from *Smile*.

Advertising mascots

Characters from adverts are also extremely popular. I've sold several PG Tips monkeys, Levi's Flat Eric, Tony the Tiger, Coco the Coco Pops monkey and Quicky the Nesquik bunny. Cuddly meerkats from Compare The Market adverts used to be popular but their value's gone down now.

A few years ago, I entered a competition with Anchor Spreadable. I didn't win the main prize, but I did get a cuddly elephant that featured in their adverts. To my surprise it was fetching around £60 on eBay because it was a limited edition.

IKEA soft toys

Some of the IKEA soft toys can be worth up to £25 each. The quirky ones, such as the badger in a doctor's uniform and a fox, are the most popular. They all have their names on their tags.

Jellycat

I love Jellycat soft toys. They're cute, extremely soft and there are so many variations and styles. They're a really popular gift for newborn babies and because they're pricey to buy new, they're always in demand. I think a lot of parents buy a replacement in case their child loses their favourite Jellycat. Many retain their value – in fact you can get up to £90 for ones that are no longer made. Have a look at jellycat.com/retired-designs and jellyexpress.co.uk for more info.

Clothes and shoes

Collaborations between brands and celebrities are normally worth something. Kate Moss did a range with Topshop a few years ago and items from that are still in demand. Second-hand Dr. Martens also have a good resale value. Brands from the 90s are currently very fashionable like Kappa, Fila and Champion. Keep your eye on current trends and see if you've got something similar in your own wardrobe. Often if a current item sells out in a store, there can be a demand for it online.

Obsolete technology

Floppy disks, ink and toner cartridges, old cameras and typewriters can all be worth selling. Cassette tapes and players, CD Walkmans and MiniDisc players are all really popular retro items and can fetch hundreds of pounds.

Furniture and homeware

It's worth having a look around your granny or your parents, house for furniture and accessories from the 1950s, 60s and 70s. Mid-century items can be worth quite a lot and there are certain brands that are always really popular like Ercol and G Plan, which will usually have the manufacturer's stamp on them. Rustic items always sell well like wooden ladders that people use as towel rails and even props for weddings.

HOW TO FIND OUT WHAT SOMETHING'S WORTH

Check the sold listings on eBay

This will give you an indication of what an item's worth, although it will only show stuff that's been sold within the last ninety days.

- ☺ Search the item by keywords or if you download the eBay app, you can scan an item's barcode if it has one.
- ☺ It will bring up similar items that are currently listed on the site. Use these prices as a guide but bear in mind that these items haven't sold.
- ☺ Refine your search so it only shows you sold listings.
- ☺ It will show the amount they've sold for in green. If there's a line through it, it means the seller has taken the best offer.

Join Facebook groups

Many popular brands have dedicated Facebook groups or communities managed by fans. My mum is on a Cath Kidston group so if she wants to sell something from her collection, she'll post a photo of it on the page to get an idea from people about how much it could be worth. Sometimes you can even sell your stuff to the members of these groups.

Is it worth selling?

Not everything is going to be worth putting on eBay. Think about the time you're going to spend listing it, the fees you'll pay and the postage. After you've taken all of that into consideration you might come away with very little money. You could bundle up similar items to make it more attractive to a buyer — for example books, clothing or even toys. You might be better selling it at a car boot or donating it to your local charity shop.

Selling at a car boot

I love a car boot sale! I used to do them as a child with my parents and we still do one every year. They're a great way to make money and have a good old clear out. The average cost of a pitch is around £5–7 per car but if you want to reduce the cost, share your pitch with a friend or family member. It's always good to have company as well as an extra set of eyes to help watch over your stall. Find car boot sales in your area by using carbootjunction.com or look on local Facebook pages, Gumtree and local newspaper listings.

• •

The main car boot season runs from March to October, but I find the most popular ones are during the school holidays and on warm, sunny days as more people come out so you're more likely to sell.

MY TOP TEN TIPS FOR A SUCCESSFUL CAR BOOT

1. Make sure you have lots of change

Someone will always want to pay with a note, so make sure that you have a decent 'float', so you don't miss out on sales.

2. Buy a waterproof ground sheet

If you don't have any tables, buy a waterproof ground sheet (you can get these in the pound stores) so you can display your items nicely on the ground. Also, if it starts to rain you can quickly pull the sheet over your stuff, so it doesn't get wet.

3. Arrive early

Arrive early to secure a good pitch, especially during the peak summer season. Car boots can be really popular and sometimes they reach capacity quickly.

4. Bring your own refreshments

Take drinks and snacks with you as it can be tempting to buy a pricey burger or coffee from a catering van. This is especially important if you're bringing your kids along.

5. Keep your valuable items close

When you're setting up your stall keep the most valuable items close to you to deter thieves.

6. Be wary of 'traders'

As soon as you pitch-up, you'll probably be swarmed by a group of people who I call 'traders'. These are the people who have stalls every week and earn a living from it. They'll only want to offer you rock bottom prices for your items so they can go and resell them for more on their own stalls. Don't feel pressured to sell to them and if they offer you a low price — just say something like 'I'll consider that if it hasn't sold by the end of the day'. That often gets them to leave your stall swiftly.

7. Don't be afraid to haggle

Most buyers will try to haggle so slightly increase the price of your items, so you end up with the price you want. For example, if you want £1 for something, price it at £1.50.

8. Keep an eye out for counterfeit money

I was once at a car boot where a woman sold an Xbox console for £60 but found out later that the £20 notes that she'd been given were fake. There's a guide on how to check banknotes on the Bank of England website — bankofengland.co.uk.

9. Always clean and check your items beforehand

Wipe down anything that looks grubby with a damp cloth and check items with batteries as they can leak. If you're selling electricals, then give them a quick test as buyers will want to make sure they're working.

10. Make up clothes bundles

If you're selling clothes, consider making them into bundles according to size. This works well for baby clothes. Clothes can be quite difficult to sell so make sure they're clean and presentable.

How much can I earn from a car boot?

It depends on what you're selling, but on average you can expect to earn around £50–150 for a few hours' work. If it's a really good turnout, then you can sometimes come away with £200 or more.

Joe's expert guide to online selling

This whole section is written by my friend Joe Stutter. He's been buying and selling online since he was fifteen so he knows how to get the most cash for your items. Thanks Joe.

• •

WHERE TO LIST ITEMS

eBay

It's where I do most of my selling and you can sell stuff to buyers across the world. It's the second biggest marketplace in the world after Amazon so you can't beat it for volume of traffic. People are sometimes put off by the fees. If you sell something you have to pay 10% of the final sale price including postage and if the buyer pays by PayPal, you also pay extra. You also pay 35p to list an item, but you can list 1,000 items a month for free, so it's unlikely you'll ever have to pay this.

I think if it generates a sale then it's better than the item sitting on another site with no interest. Also, as a personal seller you're entitled to many offers and promotions from eBay, which are emailed out to you and eBay offers both buyer and seller protection.

Facebook marketplace

Facebook created a marketplace feature so people could sell their items locally. Buyers can search within a certain radius depending on how far they want to travel. It's a good place to sell bulky items like furniture or large toys that would be difficult to post and it's also free. The buyer pays you directly so there's an element of trust there and the seller chooses whether they will deliver, or the buyer picks up.

Gumtree/Shpock

These classified ads style websites/apps are free to use with paid upgrades to make your listing more visible. Shpock is a car boot sale app where you can buy, sell or giveaway items in your area. It's free to join and there are no fees when you sell something.

Etsy

Etsy is an online marketplace specialising in handmade and vintage items.

HOW TO LIST YOUR ITEMS TO SELL

Decide what to list

Only list items that you think will sell quickly or that you'll get the most money from. Listing can be a time-consuming process and if you list low-end items, you might actually end up out of pocket after you've paid selling fees and postage. If you're selling anything for £5 or below it's probably not worth it. I generally don't put anything up for sale that's less than £10.

Think about the time of year

With some items you're going to attract more interest if you sell them at certain times of the year. For example, you might struggle to sell a paddling pool or some garden furniture in November. But if you put them up for for sale in the spring, then you'll probably get a lot of interest. Always think seasonally. Most things sell well in the run up to Christmas.

Maximise every word to make sure your title stands out

Get as much information as you can in there. For example, instead of just saying 'Mario World Nintendo 64 game', you could say 'Mario World Nintendo 64 Game boxed & complete in very good condition. Free P&P.' Use capital letters for maximum effect.

- Keep your description short, simple and to the point. Make it clear what you're selling and always be honest.
- Refer to the photos and highlight any damage, even the smallest thing, as you want to avoid disputes further down the line.
- Include measurements. This is especially important for clothes and furniture. Sometimes where the buyer doesn't need exact measurements, I use a visual prop which shows how big the item is. So, I'll photograph it next to a tin of beans or a bottle of pop.
- Test your item is working. If you're not able to, then make sure you clearly state that the item hasn't been tested.
- You might want to include extra info like 'from a smoke and pet-free home'. But only do this if it's true. I once bought some DVDs and they reeked of smoke and I had to replace all the cases.

Put it in the right category

Make sure you put your item in the right category because it can affect how the item is seen or ranked in results.

HOW TO PRICE ITEMS

Use the 'buy it now' option

A lot of people assume eBay is solely an auction site, but it's become more of a marketplace. I prefer to sell items at a set price by using the 'buy it now' option rather than having an auction. I hear so many stories of people starting auctions at 99p expecting to get a lot of bids to create a bidding war. However, unless the item is in demand or usually retails for a lot, it can be a risky move. When you consider postage and fees you could actually end up making a loss. Also, if you sell via the 'buy it now' option, you don't have to wait for an auction to end so it's a much quicker way to sell something.

Set a higher price

Set the price a little higher than you're hoping for then it can be reduced over time. It provides a bit of wiggle room for people to haggle and you want them to feel like they've got a bargain. If I want £50 for an item, I might put it on for £55–60. You can put it on even higher to test the market, but you're more likely to sell something at a realistic price.

Adjust the price

You'll always get people messaging you to make an offer. If you want to accept it, readjust your listing and then they'll probably buy it.

HOW TO TAKE GOOD PHOTOS

- ☺ Try to use natural light. Taking a photo outside or near a window always works well.
- ☺ Keep the background plain and ideally white. You could hang up a white sheet to create a plain backdrop or taking a photo of your item in the bath can work well. I tend to photo my items on a sideboard against a white wall.
- ☺ If you're selling clothes, you could try hanging them on a doorframe.
- ☺ If you can isolate the item, it always looks a lot cleaner and more professional. If you're selling a chest of drawers for example, make sure it's not covered in clutter in the photos so you can see it properly.
- ☺ I always take photos on my smartphone as they're easier to upload straight on to the eBay app.

POSTAGE AND PACKAGING

- ☺ Before you sell an item, get a rough idea of how much it's going to cost to post. It's not just the weight of an item but also its size that can make it cost more and don't forget that cardboard boxes, bubble wrap and tape can all add extra weight.
- ☺ Always opt for a tracked service so you can ensure the item has been delivered — if you have no proof it's easier for the seller to open a claim against you.
- ☺ If you're sending lots of parcels, the Post Office offers a fast-track pre-paid card service called Drop & Go where you can top-up a card with money and list how you want to send each parcel. It can then be dropped off at your local post office without queuing so it's really handy if you're busy.

FEEDBACK AND RATINGS

Always leave feedback where possible. It builds trust and can help others make an informed decision. I tend to do it once I have confirmation that the item has been received by the buyer.

REFUNDS AND RETURNS

Unfortunately, these are part of selling online. Things do go wrong sometimes whether it's your fault or not. Keep as much documentation as possible like postage receipts and photographs of your item. If an item gets lost in the post, you should be able to open a claim with the company that was supposed to deliver it but bear in mind that many have a long list of excluded items.

WHAT TO DO IF YOUR ITEMS AREN'T SELLING

- ☺ Check to see if similar items are selling.
- ☺ Make sure the price and postage combined isn't more than other sellers.
- ☺ Check that you haven't made a spelling mistake in your listing, especially in the title.
- ☺ Remember you can remove your listing at any time.

SELLING CLOTHES ONLINE

I sell my clothes online and think it's a great way to clear your wardrobe and make some money. Here are my top five places:

eBay.co.uk

One of the most popular sites to sell clothes on. See Joe's expert guide for how to do it on page 159. To work out how much profit you might make from selling your item on eBay go to finalfeecalc.co.uk.

Preloved.co.uk

This site allows you to sell items in your local area. Although clothes sell at a lower price compared to other websites, you list them for free and you can save a lot of money on postage and get instant payment on delivery.

Depop.com

Depop is an app with more than 10 million buyers and sellers. It's a bit like Instagram because you can upload a picture of the item you're selling, add a caption and buyers can like and comment on posts. As well as clothes, you can sell books, home items, jewellery and shoes. Listing is free but they charge a fee on sales (around 10%). Vintage clothes tend to sell well on here.

Vinted.co.uk

An online marketplace where you can buy, sell or swap your clothes. Selling is free but buyers need to pay a 'buyer protection' fee which ranges from 3–8% of the sale price. Good for selling high-street brands like Mango and Zara.

Rebelle.com

A site for selling designer clothes and bags. You list your item and then send it to Rebelle who will check that it's authentic. Once it's sold, they'll post the item to the buyer and transfer the money to you, minus commission. Commission is usually around 17–33% but check the website for current fees.

AMAZING MEMBERS' HACKS

'If you're selling clothes online then make sure you iron them before you take a photo. It's amazing how many people don't, and it really puts you off if they're all creased.'

'Instagram auctions are a really popular way to sell second-hand clothes. You post a photo and a short description of the item on your grid and then people make their best offer — the highest offer wins. They pay via PayPal and you post them the item.'

Some amazing members' selling stories I had to share with you . . .

As some of my Facebook members have found out, you can sometimes make more money from buying than selling. Check out these gems.

'A family member bought a watch at a car boot sale. When he took it to be repaired, he found out it was an old Rolex and was worth thousands.'

'I bought some fairy curtains at a car boot sale, but my daughter didn't like them. They sat in a bag for ages before I put them on eBay. I bought them for £2 and they sold for £26.'

'I bought a shoebox full of original Action Man accessories for £2.50 from a charity shop. One little German helmet sold for £60.'

'I bought a men's Prada raincoat in a charity shop for £9. I wasn't sure it was genuine but when I got it home, I found the serial number. I sold it on eBay for £250.'

'My daughter bought me a bag from her school fair for 50p. It had been in the cupboard for four years before I told her that I probably wasn't going to use it. So, we put it on eBay, and it sold for £60 and I gave her the money.'

And one from my dad!

My dad rescues abandoned bikes from skips and tips or buys them for a few quid off local selling sites. Once he paid just over £4 for a bike that cost over £200 new. He makes around £40 profit on each one that he sells.

Making money on your smartphone

If you've got a smartphone there are some ways that you can use it to make some extra cash.

• •

SURVEYS

Voxpopme

Earn money on Voxpopme by answering questions via video. You can earn between 25—50p for every video accepted and generally there are twenty to thirty opportunities to record videos each month. Once you reach the £10 payment threshold you can cash out via PayPal.

Swagbucks

You earn money from Swagbucks by completing surveys, watching videos and answering daily polls. The points you earn (called Swagbucks) can be exchanged for gift cards or a cash payment via PayPal.

Toluna

An app that will pay you for taking surveys. You collect points that can be spent on gift cards or rewards. You can cash out via PayPal when you reach £35 — before that you can use your earnings to get a gift card.

Fronto

This app, which is only available for Android, puts adverts on your smartphone, and you earn points for unlocking your phone screen. If you click through to the websites of the companies that are being advertised, then you can earn extra points. Points can be exchanged for gift vouchers at shops including Amazon and M&S.

YouGov

YouGov is one of the biggest market research companies. You sign up on their website and earn money for answering surveys, taking part in polls and panels. Around election times there can be lots of opportunities to give your opinion.

i-Say

Every time you complete a survey you make i-Say points. When you've collected enough points, you can redeem them as a voucher for retailers, such as Amazon, Argos and Boots.

How much can you earn from these apps?

If you have the spare time (bear in mind that some surveys can take fifteen to twenty minutes to complete), these apps are good to do to earn a little bit of extra money. But there are no guarantees about the number of surveys that you're going to get, and it can take months to build up enough cash to collect a voucher or a payout. For example, with Toluna you earn fifteen points for a one-question survey and around 2,000 points for a twenty-minute-one. To claim a £5 Starbucks voucher, you'll need to have collected 27,000 points.

TAKING STOCK PHOTOGRAPHS

Newspapers, magazines and websites buy stock photos to use in their publications — they will often be generic shots of a place or a landmark. For example, a few years ago, £50 million pounds worth of cocaine was washed up on a beach near me in Great Yarmouth. All the national newspapers reported on this and along with their stories they used a stock photograph of this local beach. The person who had taken this stock photo must have made hundreds of pounds as it was all over the news for days. So why not take your own stock photos of the area that you live in and upload them to a website? The more obscure the place, the more chance you might have of making money. There will be lots of stock photos available of the London Eye for example but there is less likely to be stock images of landmarks, monuments and parks in your local area. So, the next time you go for a walk, take a few snaps.

These sites will only accept high-resolution pictures (most new iPhones take photos that are good enough), upload it on to a website and leave it there. Your photos might never sell but if they do, you can make a couple of pounds each time someone buys one of your images. Some websites that will sell your stock photos are picfair.com, foap.com and shuttershock.com. Photos that you upload to foap.com sell for $10 each and they take 50% commission so you'll receive $5, which will be converted into GBP.

How to be a mystery shopper

I've done lots of mystery shopping over the years. It's a good way to make a little bit of extra money as well as getting free food or a night out. However, as more than 500,000 people in the UK are registered as mystery shoppers, there can be lots of competition for jobs.

• •

MY GUIDE TO MYSTERY SHOPPING

What is mystery shopping?

Most big chains use mystery shopping companies so someone can visit their business anonymously and check if their stores and staff are meeting certain standards in customer service and cleanliness. This way they get a true reflection of a customer's experience and the employees don't know that they're being assessed.

How does mystery shopping work?

☺ You enroll with one of the online companies or apps and answer a few questions. Once you've been approved, you put in your postcode and it will show you the jobs that are available in your area and you choose the ones you want to accept.

☺ You're often competing with lot of other people, especially if you live in a big city, so jobs tend to be snapped up quickly.

☺ Before you do the task, you'll be sent specific instructions. They will tell you what questions to ask, what items or products you need to buy and any photos you need to take.

☺ They'll also send you a detailed list of the things you need to look out for and report back on, such as the cleanliness of the store, whether someone greeted you when you walked in, the lighting in the store and the customer service.

☺ Then you'll choose a date to complete your shop and they'll tell you when you need to submit your report.

☺ The company you're working for will let you know what you'll be reimbursed for and the fee that you'll be paid.

☺ Afterwards you'll need to fill out quite a detailed report about your experience.

☺ When you submit the report, you'll have to wait for a few weeks (possibly four or more) to be reimbursed for anything that you paid for and to receive your fee.

What skills do you need to become a mystery shopper?

1. A good memory – you'll need to remember quite a lot of information so you can put it in your report.
2. An eye for detail – you could be asked to comment on anything from the layout of the shop to the cleanliness and the lighting to what the person who served you was wearing.
3. Be available – you should have enough time to visit the shop or conduct the survey and write a detailed report afterwards.

4. Be factual and professional — mystery shopping isn't about giving your personal opinion. It's about providing a factual report about your experience.
5. Keep things confidential — when you carry out your tasks, remember staff are not supposed to know that you're a mystery shopper. You shouldn't talk about surveys or mystery visits afterwards either.

How much do mystery shoppers make?

It's definitely not a way to get rich quick and you would struggle to get enough jobs to earn a living from it. It's a good way to make a little bit of extra money. It also depends on how many assignments you do. You can be paid anything from £5 to £12 per job although some companies pay more. A lot of mystery shoppers do it mainly to get the free meals and other products as the pay is minimal. Callum and I have had meals out at four-star restaurants where we got £60 worth of food for free and got paid £5 on top of that. Other assignments have involved ordering takeaway pizza at home. I've mystery shopped for supermarkets where you have to go into a store and ask an employee a particular question and report back on how they dealt with you. I've also had to go into a betting shop and put a bet on. The bonus with this one was that I won the bet and I could keep my winnings!

Other assignments can be very short and are much quicker and simpler to complete but you won't earn as much for them. So, you might have to go into a store, take a photo of a certain product on a shelf and then upload it to an app.

Things to be aware of

If the job involves eating out, be mindful of how much your allowance is. If you're only getting £20 reimbursed, then any extra that you spend will end up coming out of your own pocket. If the allowance is low, you might only get a free meal for one person so if you take someone else with you, you'll have to pay for that yourself.

It sounds easy but it can be quite hard work. If you're having a meal out, then I find it hard to relax because you've got to remember every single detail for your report. Making notes on my phone helps.

Where to find mystery shopping jobs

My favourite websites to apply for mystery shopping jobs are:
Marketforce – uk.marketforceshopper.com
Redwigwam – redwigwam.com
Grassroots – grassrootsmysteryshopping.com
BeMyEye app

EVER THOUGHT ABOUT STARTING YOUR OWN BUSINESS?

Last year, after a holiday of a lifetime to Disney World, **Vicky Ferguson (talesoftoriasoaps.co.uk)** decided to take the plunge and set up her own business selling Disney-inspired soaps, bath bombs and beauty. If you've got a small business idea and are thinking about taking the plunge, here's her advice.

⊚ Introduce yourself to your customers and your followers. Since starting my own business, I've bought from so many more small businesses because I've got to know them as people. Shopping small means customers get to build this connection with the business owner which you don't often get on the high street. Including yourself in your social media posts, doing live streams or just showing your personality in your post descriptions or bio can really help.

☺ Connecting with your customers is super important. All my new followers get a direct message welcoming them to my journey and asking for any ideas. It's simple but it gets them engaged.

☺ Make sure you genuinely love what you're doing. It's something you'll be spending a lot of time on so it's so important that it makes you happy. People can tell if you have a genuine passion for your product and it encourages them to buy it.

☺ Start small. Don't overdo it. I find it best to start with a smaller collection of products that you know are perfect and then gradually introduce more. Often people find that having too much choice is daunting. Set some goals regarding sales, income and where you would like to be in a few months' time. It's great for your mindset to see how far you've come.

☺ Packaging is important. To me, buying an item from a small business is like giving yourself a present, so it's important to present it well. I also like to add my own little touch to each package. So, all my parcels are hand-stamped with my logo and include an organic teabag and some biodegradable flower petals. Come up with your own personal touch. Giving your customers that little bit of excitement when they open their mail will encourage them to return.

☺ Check your stock, then check it again. There have been so many times when I've been packaging orders and realised that I've sold a bath bomb that I actually don't have so I have to quickly make up a new batch. I now list less than what I actually have in stock, so that way if I need to replace an order, I still have the item there available.

⊚ Connect with other small businesses. This will give you a support network to fall back on. I created a group for other small businesses that make Disney-related items and the support each of us has received from one another has been invaluable. They will also share your shop, which will bring their customers over to you and vice versa.

Do you have a story to share?

Everyone has a story to tell but what a lot of people don't realise is that the things that have happened in your own life could be fascinating to someone else and that you could earn money from selling your story to newspapers and magazines. I should know — I've done it myself! So, here's my guide to how to sell your story to the UK press for cash. There are a number of ways you can get your story into print.

NEWS AGENCIES

Agencies act as a middleman between you and newspapers and magazines. If you contact them, they will approach several different publications on your behalf and try to sell your story to the highest bidder or your preferred newspaper or magazine. They have good contacts with the news and commissioning editors at these publications and they will be able to tell you if your story is likely to be of interest.

They will be paid by the publication for selling them your story (sometimes this is a separate fee to yours), but the good thing about agencies is that they can do multiple deals on your behalf. If there's enough interest, they might be able to place your story in several different publications earning you a fee for each one and even organise TV interviews if that's something you want to do.

Some reputable news agencies include:
PA Media — pa.media/sell-your-story
Cavendish Press — cavendish-press.co.uk
Sell My Story — sellmystory.co.uk
Talk to the Press — talktothepress.co.uk
HotSpot Media — hotspotmedia.co.uk

What will happen if they like my story?

If an agency thinks your story has potential, they'll arrange a phone call with you to get more information. If they decide to pitch to the press and it's successful, they will offer you a fee for your story and arrange a date and time for you to be interviewed (and possibly photographed) for the feature.

REAL-LIFE MAGAZINES

Real-life weekly magazines are always on the lookout for true stories and they'll pay a fee for them. Most magazines have forms on their websites that you can fill in and submit, or an email address that you can send a summary of your story to. Make sure you include your email address and mobile number and try to keep it short and to the point.
If they are interested, a writer from the magazine's features team will get in contact with you.

Some weekly magazines who take real-life stories include:
Thatslife.co.uk
Takeabreak.co.uk
Realpeoplemag.co.uk
Bellamagazine.co.uk
Womansown.co.uk

NEWSPAPERS

Newspapers are always looking for good stories. They're more interested in news and current events than magazines but they will also have women's and lifestyle sections that will often feature real-life stories. You can also send them videos, pictures and tip-offs if you have a good story that's not about you but that you think might be worth them looking into. They all have designated phone numbers and email addresses on their websites so you can email, text or phone them with your story or tip-offs.

You could try:
exclusive@the-sun.co.uk
mirrornews@mirror.co.uk
tips@dailymail.com
newsdesk@independent.co.uk

FACEBOOK GROUPS

There are Facebook groups set up by freelance journalists who use them to try to find case studies for features that they're writing for various publications. It can be anything from looking for volunteers to test out a new beauty treatment or the latest craze to setting someone up on a blind date or talking to them about their weight loss or their husband's affair. They're definitely worth joining in case you fit the bill for any of their requests and you want to take part in a feature. One of the biggest ones is FeatureMe! UK.

How much money can you make?

How much money you get for your story will depend on several factors.

☺ Demand — if lots of magazines and newspapers want your story then there will potentially be a bidding war and you will get a higher fee.

☺ Exclusivity — if your story is exclusive to one publication you might get paid more.

Some other things to bear in mind

Your story must be true, and it will also be subject to legal checks. If it involves someone else, then the publication might have to approach the other person to give them their 'right of reply'. Publications rarely do anonymous stories so you must be willing to use your full name and for them to use your photograph and of any of the people involved in your story. The only exception to this is if you're involved in a court case and your identification is protected by law. On average you can expect to earn between £200 and £800 for a full feature, but if your story is particularly in demand or topical then you can potentially earn thousands of pounds.

How I sold my story

Several years ago, I'd just split up with my boyfriend and moved into a new flat. I was still at college studying animal care part-time and I spent a lot of money on petrol driving the two hours there and back several times a week. My rent was £450 a month and one month, I was really short. I was in such a pickle but didn't want to ask my parents to bail me out.

I racked my brains about what I could do to make some extra cash to be able meet the rent. One day I was reading a weekly true-life magazine and there was a story in it about a woman who had fifteen cats and how she was a crazy cat lady. At the time, I was obsessed with rats. I used to adopt rats that had been badly treated in the entertainment industry and I had eighteen at one point. If she was a crazy cat lady, then why couldn't I be a crazy rat lady? So, I filled in the form that was in the magazine and told them how I was nineteen years old and had eighteen rats that were like my children. I sent the form off and a few days later a journalist called me to say they wanted to feature my story in the magazine. I ended up getting paid £300 — enough to help me out with my rent that month.

It proved to me that I could make money from selling my story, so I decided to talk about the horrible time I'd had with bullies when I was a teenager. This time I went through a news agency and over two years they placed my story in three different magazines and I earned £2,000. It was an upsetting thing to talk about and being interviewed was hard, but in a way, it gave me closure. I also wanted to speak out to help other kids who were perhaps going through something similar and show them that in the end, things would get better. I was worried about the reaction I'd get from other people and I had a few comments, but overall everyone was really supportive.

If you have a story, why not think about sharing it with the press? It could help other people who are going through something similar, raise awareness of a charity or medical condition or even help promote your business, brand or website as well as earn you some extra cash along the way.

Story-sharing tips

Look for the hashtag, journorequest on Twitter. Journalists use it to search for case studies for newspapers and magazines and it's a way of finding out what media opportunities are available.

Not all media opportunities are paid but they still might be worth doing if you have a blog or a business to promote.

Ask if the article can include a link to your website or blog as it's a good opportunity to pick up new followers.

Get the publication to show you your story or quotes before it's published — including the headline — so you can check that everything is correct and you're happy with it. Sometimes they won't be able to email you your story for legal reasons but ask if they can read it through to you over the phone instead.

How to become an influencer

I never set out to become an 'influencer'. My passion was always hunting out the best bargains and letting people know about them. Eventually I realised rather than telling people about what I'd found, it would be so much easier if I could take my phone with me and actually show them the bargains on the shop shelf instead. That's why, six years ago, I started my YouTube channel. At the time, not many people were vlogging outside their homes and I was one of the first people to film myself going into stores. Now the influencer market has exploded and so many people want to be part of it. In fact, a recent survey showed that one in five children want a career as a social media influencer. So, if you're just starting out or if you're thinking about giving YouTube a go, here's my advice.

• •

MY TOP TIPS IF YOU WANT TO START A YOUTUBE CHANNEL

Find your niche

This is one of the most important things. Don't go on YouTube trying to be someone else. You can only truly excel at it if it's something that you're passionate about. There's no point trying to be the next Zoella if you don't like beauty. I go out and film myself finding bargains because I love bargain hunting. Sometimes it can take a while to find your 'thing'. One of my friends started off doing bargain shopping videos like me but then she realised she enjoyed doing lifestyle and body confidence videos more. There's even a guy who films himself cleaning swimming pools — his videos get hundreds of thousands of views and it's just him doing his day job.

Be yourself

Don't be afraid to show your personality and develop your own style. When I first started making videos, I felt I needed to be like a children's TV presenter, and I was so OTT — in fact I cringe when I look back at some of my earlier videos! Don't feel like you've got to put on a posh voice or speak a certain way — people want to see a real person and feel connected to you.

Learn to be comfortable in front of the camera

This takes time — I know I certainly wasn't comfortable at first. Film a few trial videos and show them to your family and friends. Someone I know filmed a video every single day for a week. They didn't publish them and at the end of the week, they watched their first video and their last and figured out where they needed to change. It's about getting to know yourself. Because of my autism, I really struggle with filming videos where it's just me talking straight into the camera. But if I'm in my car and I'm doing a vlog I'll sometimes have a quick chat and it feels more relaxed than being sat at home with a camera pointing at me. You don't even have to be in front of the camera all of the time to be successful. In many of my videos when I'm out shopping, I don't even show my face.

You don't need expensive equipment

If you're just starting out, then your smartphone will be fine for filming videos. Perhaps when you're getting around 2,000–5,000 views per video and you're starting to see earnings from your channel, you might want to invest in a camera, but it's not essential. A good thing to invest in is a ring light, especially if you're going to be making a lot of videos from home where you're talking straight into the camera. You can pick these up cheaply on Amazon and eBay.

Things don't need to be perfect

I struggle with this because I'm a perfectionist, but your videos don't need to be perfect. Things will go wrong and I've learnt over time that people like it when that happens. So now if there are any disasters or we make mistakes, I tend to leave them in. All sorts of things have happened when we've been filming from things falling off the shelves to items tipping over. Once I stood in some chewing gum which viewers thought was hilarious.

Be prepared to work hard

People think it's easy but a heck of a lot of work goes into being an influencer. I only post one video a week. When I'm in a store filming, I'm out on average for five hours. I then have about two hours' of content that I edit down to ten minutes and the editing can take me three hours. One short video takes me a good eight hours' of work.

Follow the guidelines

YouTube issues a whole list of guidelines that you should go through before you decide to become a content creator.

Always check who is visible in your videos and remember to blur people's faces out, especially children.

Look what's going on in the background

Sometimes I'm so focused on what I'm filming and the great bargains I've found that I don't notice what's going on in the background. I once filmed some alphabet candles and didn't notice that someone had spelt out an offensive word with them. I only realised when I posted the video online and started getting loads of comments and quickly had to take it down. Another time there was a woman swearing loudly in the background of one of my videos. I'd only filmed one take so it meant I couldn't use it. Now every time I film an item for one of my videos, I do three or four takes of the same thing.

Develop a thick skin

If you put yourself on social media, then you will probably get criticism and negative comments and it can be hard. I don't want to turn the comments off because it helps your engagement to interact with followers, so now I just ignore them. My friend Connor helps to moderate my comments and deletes anything he thinks might upset me. There's also a setting where you can filter out certain words and hide certain people's comments. If you're an influencer, then you're going to get some negativity so don't engage with trolls and over time you will develop a thick skin.

Be patient

Don't expect everything to happen overnight. It takes time to grow and you'll have to work for it. I'm approaching 100,000 followers on YouTube and that's taken me six years. It took three years before I was getting a significant number of views.

Use hashtags

You can put up to three hashtags in a description so do use them all as they can help. But keep it simple. If I do a video in Home Bargains for example, I'll hashtag it #homebargains, #homebargainshaul and #Hollyvlogs. You can also add hashtags when you're uploading the video to YouTube.

Use short, snappy titles

Make the titles of your videos short and to the point. If you come up in people's suggested box or they search for you, you want them to instantly see what your video is about. You only see the first 50 characters on Google so if your title is too long, it will cut it off.

You can use shock tactics to get people to click on your videos although I don't like to do this too often. We filmed one video where we broke down three times on the way home from a bargain store, so I called it 'you won't believe what just happened.' Sometimes shock titles (also known as clickbait) can work well to get people to click on the video but make sure the title represents the content otherwise viewers get annoyed.

Interact with your subscribers

It's so important to interact with people following you. If someone has taken the time to comment on one of my videos I always try to respond, even if it's just liking their comment.

Look at the trends

In social media there are always trends. I will take something that's trending and do my own version of it. At one point, people were looking at Trip Advisor for the

worst-rated hotel in their area and then staying there.
Callum and I did this and filmed a video. The hotel was filthy,
and Callum was convinced it was haunted. It was that bad I
didn't stay there but Callum did and made a fun video.
If you're struggling for content ideas, then have a look at
what's trending on YouTube and put your own spin on it.

OTHER THINGS THAT CAN HELP

Get the YouTube creator Studio app

This is a really handy tool and it's so much easier than
using it on a desktop. It means you can interact easily
with subscribers.

Subscription services

There are services that will give you tools to help you grow
your channel. TubeBuddy will pool information about your
competitors! It will tell you the hashtags they're using and
other useful info. There's a free basic version and the
subscription service starts at $9 a month.

Get your name across all platforms

Keep your username short and simple and get it across all
platforms as well as YouTube even if you don't necessarily
use them. My username is @hollyvlogs but I didn't grab it on
TikTok in time and when I tried, it was already taken so I'm
@hollyvlogsofficial on there. You can reach more people, and
different kinds of people, if you're on several platforms.

How you make money from YouTube

You've got to have around 4,000 hours' worth of watch time
within a year and 1,000 subscribers before you can start to

'monetise' your channel — which means you make money from adverts on your channel. Google automatically places adverts on your videos and every month, when you reach £60 or more, you'll get a payment from Google.

YouTubers earn the majority of their money from brand deals. The rates brands pay depend on your channel size, engagement and average views per video. Brands will pay to advertise across all your social media accounts.

Affiliate marketing is another way influencers can earn money. You get a small bit of commission every time you generate a sale for a brand. If you do regular haul videos this can add up.

How much I make

Don't go on YouTube expecting to be famous and to make loads of money. I had my channel for years without making a penny and I did it because I enjoyed it. I certainly don't make millions from it now. On a good month I earn around £500–1,200 in advertising revenue depending on how many videos I make.

I try to post one video a week and on average each of my videos will earn around £100 in the first month. My most popular video was when I challenged myself to spend £100 in Poundland. It's had 500,000 views and it's made around £900 to date.

My videos are time sensitive. If I have a video on bargains, I've found in Poundland in July 2020 then it's not going to get many views over the following years. But if you've got a lifestyle channel, you might make videos that people can watch for years and they'll keep making you money.

My first brand deal on YouTube was for Graze box when I had 2,000 subscribers and I earned £150. When I had 35,000 subscribers, I got £900 from a suntan lotion company and the most recent brand deal I did was for a £2,500 fee. It's really important to only work with brands that you believe in and products that you genuinely love and also make it clear in your posts that it's an advert or a sponsored post.

TIKTOK

In the past year, TikTok's popularity has exploded, especially with the younger generation and it's the fastest growing social media platform in the world. Compared to YouTube, things grew quickly for me on TikTok. After two years I have more than 400,000 followers. I gained 300,000 of those followers in six months after a series of videos I made on TikTok got over a million views each and went viral.

Why I love TikTok

It's quick. The videos you post are short. They can be anything up to 60 seconds, but the ideal length is around 15 seconds. It's so easy to do. If you see something funny you can just pick up your phone and film it.

Anything goes when it comes to content. A lot of people think TikTok is all about the dances, but I've never done a TikTok dance in my life. You can post anything and everything — from comedy videos to educational stuff and you can be really creative.

I realised I could post my bargains on there, but the one that went viral for me was when I grew a grow-your-own shark toy from Home Bargains in my bathtub. I got 100,000 new followers overnight from this one TikTok.

As well as shopping videos, I also do relatable comedy. For example, I did a TikTok saying how people could save money by taking their kids to Pets at Home instead of the zoo. People loved it because it was relatable, and it got thousands of views.

How you earn money

You earn money by getting brand deals. I've only had a couple of brand deals on TikTok. A company approached me to unbox their toys on camera and paid me £800.

EXPERT INFLUENCER HACKS!

Demi Donnelly has over 200,000 subscribers to her YouTube channel with the same name. These are her tips for you:

☺ My number one piece of advice is be yourself. In my opinion there's nothing worse than watching a video of someone that isn't being their true self and viewers can always tell.

☺ Consistency is the key to growing your following. Always have set posting days and times and stick to them so your viewers know when to check back for new content.

☺ Don't get into it for money. Yes, this is now my full-time job and you can make great money, however, you need to have a genuine love for editing and entertaining people.

Harriette Rose has over 72,000 YouTube subscribers on her channel and this is how she suggests you can make money as an influencer:

- ☺ When you're not posting videos, make sure you keep your followers interacting with you through other social media platforms. Instagram is fab for that.

- ☺ Plan your content. I plan my videos two weeks in advance. I use a desk planner and put them on sticky notes then I can swap and change videos around.

- ☺ Post regularly. On Instagram I try to post three times a day on my feed. But if you don't have any content to post then don't stress about it. Sometimes it's nice to have a break.

Fleur Roberts (@Fleur.Roberts) is only eighteen years old and she has over a million followers on TikTok! This is what she advises:

- ☺ Never give up. We've all got to start somewhere and you're not gonna just wake up with 100,000 followers.

- ☺ Stay consistent and post what you love.

- ☺ Try to be original. Post content that other people haven't already done to make yourself stand out.

And finally, here is **Morgan James** who is only twenty-one and has hundreds of thousands of followers on **TikTok** (**@morganmjames**) too.

- ☺ Don't get too obsessed with views or likes. It's hard, but I try to focus on making the best content I can.

- ☺ Have fun! If you're having fun making content, then hopefully your audience will have fun watching it too.

- ☺ Make videos that you would want to watch yourself then other people will watch them too.

- ☺ The main aim for TikTok creators is to get on the 'For You' page. To do this, follow trends and use popular hashtags.

A thank you from me

I hope that you've enjoyed reading this book. Most of all, whatever your financial situation, I hope that it's helped you in some way. Whether that's making a start to get out of debt, saving you a bit of extra cash each week or trying some of the hacks and tips that will hopefully make life a little bit easier for you and your family.

This book is just the tip of the iceberg when it comes to saving money. I'm always learning and scouring the Internet for the best tips and advice which I'll continue to share across my social media channels. I'd love to hear from you too. So, if you've managed to save or make money as a result of this book, head over to my social media and let me know.

Love

Holly x

Acknowledgements

First up I'd like to thank my family. Mum and Dad — even though I hated Dad's extreme cheapskate ways, it taught me a lot! And started my love for money saving.

To my husband Callum, thanks for being supportive of my frugal lifestyle. And Mollie and Bella for understanding the 'luxuries' we get in life (such as Disney World trips) are due to cutting back on spends throughout the year. Even at your young age you know the value of money and hopefully Cloud will grow up to be frugal too.

Two very important people I would like to thank . . .

Joe Stutter who started as a friend and is now my business partner. I can't thank you enough for everything you have done for me over the years (even back in our teens when you helped me make fan websites for my favourite celebrities!). I always knew you would be a successful entrepreneur and I couldn't have picked anyone better to run my business with.

Joseph Tirelli of JT Marketing PR. Thank you for picking up the phone back in 2015 and listening to my wild idea of pulling off the world's biggest coupon shop. Most people would have thought I was crazy, but you had faith in me. Thanks to you, Paula and even your wife Shirley for putting up with the late nights you spent working on projects for me. *Grazie, non avrei potuto farlo senza di te.*

Thank you to the admin team on the Extreme Couponing and Bargains UK Facebook Group. Freyja, Sammy, Kayleigh and

Lorraine, thank you for dedicating your time to making the group a safe and enjoyable place for 1.3 million members.

Thank you to Laura Higginson at Penguin for believing in me, Heather Bishop for helping to turn my words into reality, Linda Blacker for an amazing cover shoot and Laura Edwards and Alex at the Viral Group for making this book happen.

A final thanks to all of my friends – the YouTubers, vloggers, bloggers, influencers and TikTok stars who have been so supportive of this book and who have taken the time to share their expert knowledge with me. A big thank you to Nicola at the frugalcottage.com, Kelly at reducedgrub.com, Iwan at mrcarrington.co.uk, Kate McCabe, Amy Coombes, Jonathan Gutteridge at themoneyshed.co.uk, Leigh and Nick from The Lodge Guys, Stephie and Dave from Krispy Smore, Luke and Rich from L&R Dreaming, Francesca from themoneyfox. com, Donna from savvymumuk.co.uk, Katy Stevens from katykicker.com, Tom Bryant from magicfreebies.co.uk, Demi Donnelly, Harriette Rose, Fleur Roberts and Morgan James.

Index

Notes

Notes

Notes

Ebury Press, an imprint of Ebury Publishing,
20 Vauxhall Bridge Road,
London SW1V 2SA

Ebury Press is part of the Penguin Random House group of companies
whose addresses can be found at global.penguinrandomhouse.com

Penguin
Random House
UK

First published by Ebury Press in 2020

www.penguin.co.uk

A CIP catalogue record for this book is available from the British Library

Text Design: Two Associates
Typeset by Jouve
Plate section photography: Steve Painter
Styling by Rebecca Woods

ISBN 9781529108187

Printed and bound in Great Britain by Clays Ltd, Elcograf S.p.A.

MIX
Paper from
responsible sources
FSC® C016897

Penguin Random House is committed to a sustainable future for our
business, our readers and our planet. This book is made from
Forest Stewardship Council® certified paper.

Disclaimer

All information and links in this book were correct at the time of going to
press. I wrote this book in 2020 during the Covid-19 global crisis. My
hope is that all my tips, which I have used for years, remain relevant as
we come out of lockdown. If you find that anything in this book is not
possible, please let me know. I'll be keeping a close eye on changes too
and will add a note on my website at extremecouponing.co.uk/book if
anything changes.